# FRANK GEHRY Toronto

Edited by Dennis Reid

Art Gallery of Ontario, Toronto

The Art Gallery of Ontario is partially funded by the Ontario Ministry of Culture. Additional operating support is received from the Volunteers of the Art Gallery of Ontario, City of Toronto, the Department of Canadian Heritage and the Canada Council for the Arts.

This book is published on the occasion of *Frank Gehry: Art + Architecture*, an exhibition organized by the Art Gallery of Ontario, February 18 – May 7, 2006.

Supported by the Canada Council for the Arts  Canada Council for the Arts   Conseil des Arts du Canada

Library and Archives Canada Cataloguing in Publication

Frank Gehry : Toronto / edited by Dennis Reid.
ISBN 1-894243-49-8

1. Gehry, Frank O., 1929-.  2. Gehry, Frank O., 1929- --Interviews.
3. Architecture--20th century.  I. Reid, Dennis  II. Art Gallery of Ontario

NA737.G44F73 2006          720'.92          C2005-907856-1

Editing: Catherine van Baren, Design Studio, AGO
Graphic design: Aleksandra Grzywaczewska, Design Studio, AGO
Production: Karen Sung, Design Studio, AGO
Printing: Bowne of Toronto
Typography: FF MetaPlusBook, Trade Gothic

Printed in Canada

Cover
Architectural drawings of the sculpture promenade.
Photo: Courtesy of Gehry Partners, LLP

Title Page
Frank Gehry
Photo: Thomas Mayer

Art Gallery of Ontario
317 Dundas Street West
Toronto, Ontario, Canada M5T 1G4
www.ago.net

# FRANK GEHRY
## Toronto


Foreword by Matthew Teitelbaum   4

Frank Gehry: The Early Years by Gillian MacKay   8

A Century of Building the Art Gallery of Ontario by Dennis Reid   22

Frank Gehry: Seeing the AGO Again (and Again) by Larry Wayne Richards   38

In School with Frank Gehry by George Baird   56

Model Employee by An Te Liu   60

Object Lessons by Michael Mantzoris   64

Refinements in Radical Form-making: The View from within Gehry's Office, 1999–2001 by Tom Bessai   68

Contributors   71

# Foreword

It is easy to think of Frank Gehry simply as an architect/sculptor who creates space as beautiful form. The exteriors of the radiant Guggenheim Museum in Bilbao, Spain, the exuberant Walt Disney Concert Hall in Los Angeles, even the modest Maggie's Centre in Dundee, Scotland, all speak to the expressive qualities of finish and form. Such buildings, seen but not experienced, can easily lead to simplifications in understanding Gehry's achievements. To walk through one of his buildings, and around it, is to experience a sense of discovery while passing through its spaces and understanding how its design responds to the specifics of its site and surroundings.

In the five years we have known and worked with him at the Art Gallery of Ontario, I have come to understand Gehry not as a theoretical architect who imposes ideas on a site, but as an analytical problem-solver who applies imaginative ideas to the specifics of a challenge. From the beginning Gehry insistently asked about our needs and programs, because he wanted to design from the inside out – the outside form would be an expression of what happens inside. He wanted to create a journey linked inextricably to the gallery in which the art would be seen. It was clear he wanted an open and inviting Art Gallery of Ontario, one that strengthens the relationship between art and architecture, the

Matthew Teitelbaum
Michael and Sonja Koerner Director, and CEO
Art Gallery of Ontario

Gallery and the city, and visitors and artworks.

The four other projects featured in *Frank Gehry: Art + Architecture* – the Ray and Maria Stata Center at the Massachusetts Institute of Technology in Boston, Millennium Park Music Pavilion (Jay Pritzker Pavilion) and Great Lawn in Chicago, the Walt Disney Concert Hall in Los Angeles, and the DZ Bank in Berlin – have all in some way influenced our own project. Gehry has used his own intense engagement with art and artists to create spaces that satisfy a central rule of architecture: deliver the essential promise and ensure that it works in its most fundamental sense. Just as the Walt Disney Concert Hall is a wondrous conduit for the L.A. Philharmonic, our galleries will be showcases for our Tom Thomsons and Rebecca Horns.

*Frank Gehry: Toronto* is a book we have published to accompany the exhibition *Frank Gehry: Art + Architecture*, rather than an exhibition catalogue. We have chosen to set a wider context and, to a degree, a new one, at least in emphasis. The richness of the exhibition and publication have been achieved with the involvement of many at the Art Gallery of Ontario, the University of Toronto and Gehry Partners, LLP. Four people have led this project from the start, each contributing key elements to its realization: Dennis Reid, director of Collections and Research at the AGO; George Baird, dean of the Faculty of Architecture, Landscape and Design at the University of Toronto; Larry Richards, professor of Architecture at the Faculty of Architecture, Landscape and Design at the University of Toronto, and Keith Mendenhall, Gehry Partners, LLP.

From the outset we had set ourselves the goal of looking at this exhibition as a collaboration between the gallery, the studio and the university in the belief that by asking students to help us conceive and structure the exhibition, we would see Gehry's achievement as both process and result. We would also be able to present elements of selected Gehry projects from the point of view of the curious, engaged student. We believe we have achieved this, wonderfully.

It is a pleasure to close with a warm acknowledgement of SAS Institute (Canada) Inc., the lead sponsor of *Frank Gehry: Art + Architecture*. Their generous support of this exhibition is a testament to the dedication that many individuals, corporations and foundations have demonstrated as we move forward with *Transformation AGO*. ◼

Toronto, as everyone knows, is where Frank Gehry was born and raised. The nice guy Canadian thing is one of his shticks, and he likes to play it up.

O'Keefe's
WHITE BROS
CREDIT CLOTHIERS
BOSTON LUNCH
SODA FOUNTAIN
M. JOEL FUR
RAW AND DRESSED FURS
DR BROWN
DENTIST
CAR STOP

# Frank Gehry: The Early Years

Gillian MacKay

Last September at the 2005 Toronto International Film Festival, Frank Gehry, a compact man with a shock of white hair and bright blue eyes, stepped before the microphone at the Elgin Theatre. The occasion was the opening of *Sketches of Frank Gehry*, a documentary by the celebrated Hollywood director Sydney Pollack. Flashing his broad, affable grin, Gehry thanked Pollack, who is an old friend. Then he added, to the delight of the Toronto crowd: "It's doubly, triply, quadruply great that this is being premiered in my home town – in my home and native land."

Toronto, as everyone knows, is where Frank Gehry was born and raised. The nice guy Canadian thing is one of his shticks, and he likes to play it up: witness the tiny white snowflake pin of the Companion of the Order of Canada glinting against his black blazer. On a good day, such as today, he loves Canada: loves hockey players, loves liberal politics, loves his Toronto cousins, loves wood. On a bad day, he grumbles about lack of big-think, lack of support for heroes, lack of money to make the kind of splash that visionary architects like to make.

Gehry worried throughout the film screening about whether or not people would like it. He needn't have: the film was well received by film critics and popular with the opening day audience. The sizeable crowd at the Elgin included patrons Ken and Marilyn Thomson, with whom he was photographed arm-in-arm in the lobby of the theatre, fellow architects from Gehry

Partners in Los Angeles, and a sizeable contingent from the Art Gallery of Ontario, where a major redesign of the building by Gehry is now under construction.

Gehry will be seventy-nine when the new building opens in 2008. Although his vital, almost boyish, presence and his undiminished productivity make the question of age seem irrelevant, this is probably the only building he will ever design in the city of his birth. As a matter of emotion and pride he needs to get it right. To that end he spends the better part of the day of the film premiere in meetings with gallery staff to refine such details as gallery lighting, flooring and trim finish.

A gently curving swath of glass frontage backed by a scaffolding of wooden ribs, the façade of the Gehry-designed Art Gallery of Ontario suggests the belly of a ship or the world of ice hockey. It may surprise those who know only such signature buildings as the Guggenheim Museum Bilbao or the Walt Disney Concert Hall in Los Angeles that Gehry's AGO will look nothing like those swooping flights of exuberance. Yet Gehry is not simply, or primarily, a maker of sculptural icons; he is an architect who works within the urban fabric.

In Toronto, that context is the old Jewish ghetto, which also happens to be the main stage of Gehry's childhood. The two-storey, red-brick house of his maternal grandparents at 15 Beverley Street, just down the street from the AGO, provided shelter from many a storm. He played as a child in Grange Park, and a winter walk on its snowy paths can still transport him back to his boyhood.

At the age of eight, with his mother, Frank visited the gallery for the first time. It was here at the Art Gallery of Toronto (as it was named then) that he had his first conscious experience of a work of art – a seascape, perhaps by John Marin – and of architecture itself. Walker Court, he recalls as "inspiring – awe-inspiring probably." In the redesign, it made sentimental and practical sense to him to restore Walker Court as the focal point of the main entrance. The shift eastward in the 1993 renovation had, in his view, been a mistake. "It screwed up the enfilade and the comprehension," he says. "The logic seemed to me right from the beginning to re-establish that axis that was so compelling to me when I was a kid. And when we took that tack, it seemed to organize everything again."

Once asked by a group of University of Toronto architecture students to describe the look of Toronto architecture, Gehry replied with a single word: "Homey." Returning to his roots, he has met the long-unresolved challenge of making the Art Gallery of Ontario at home in the evolving downtown neighbourhood. The original 1918–35 beaux-arts building complex, which included the old Grange house, was a fenced-in WASP enclave marooned in an East European village. Later versions of the building, cased in concrete and brick, had a somewhat fortress-like look about them.

By contrast, the new transparent façade will reflect the massed, brick Victorian houses across Dundas Street, and the glass will curve back subtly at the top to prevent it from overshadowing the streetscape. A second-floor sculpture gallery and promenade behind the glass will be visible from the street, thus opening up the building from the inside to the outside. As Gehry elaborates, "The walkway behind the glass will be lit up at night, so that the people living across the road will feel that there is life on the other side of the street. I think all that's my response to the neighbourhood."

It is generally agreed that Los Angeles, where he moved with his family in 1947, made Frank Gehry an architect. Yet Toronto remains the site of deep memory. Even today, being tapped on the shoulder by a long-lost schoolmate or singing "The Maple Leaf Forever" at his old public school surprise him by reducing him to tears. Certain of Gehry's oft-noted qualities – his appetite for life, his populist sympathies, his sudden shifts between vulnerability and pugnacity – all have their roots in a rich, but troubled Canadian childhood.


Frank Gehry was born Frank Owen Goldberg on February 28, 1929, at Toronto General Hospital.[1]

The city itself was just shy of its hundredth birthday, and it was then, as now, enjoying a growth spurt. Toronto's population had grown to 818,000 from 611,000 in the 1920s. A host of new buildings, completed or underway, including Union Station (1925), Maple Leaf Gardens (1931), the Art Gallery of Toronto (1926) and the Imperial Bank of Commerce (1929–31; noteworthy for a time as the tallest building in the British Empire), bore witness to post-war prosperity and civic optimism. Although that bubble was about to burst, the city must have looked like a civilized, hopeful place for a young couple such as Irving and Thelma Goldberg to raise their first and only son.

For much of the past century, Toronto had provided a home to Jewish immigrants such as themselves. In 1931 there were 46,000 Jews residing in Toronto compared with 3,100 in 1901. Frank's mother, Thelma, was eight when she immigrated in 1913 with her brother Kalman and her parents Samuel and Leah Caplan. Angered by anti-Semitism in his native Poland – Frank recalls his grandfather's vivid descriptions of the injustices he had endured – Samuel sold his successful coal delivery business in Lodz and moved to Toronto to join his brothers and sisters (ultimately, there would be seven).

Samuel Caplan opened a hardware store at 366 Queen Street West, just east of Spadina Avenue. He prospered sufficiently to buy a house nearby on

Beverley Street and to provide music lessons for his only daughter, a rare privilege at the time. Thelma's lively intelligence expressed itself in a love of art, music and theatre and in a yearning to study law, a desire that was not to be gratified until she was in her sixties.

Irving Goldberg, Frank's father, came to Toronto from New York City as an adult. His own father, a tailor, had died when he was young, leaving a family of nine children to shift for themselves on the streets of Hell's Kitchen. Creative in an unfocussed sort of way, Irving worked in grocery and hardware stores, then in the carny business. He once won a prize for a window display at the Canadian National Exhibition, an arrangement of foods in the form of the American flag later described by his son as "a proto-Jasper Johns." More importantly, the restless, good-looking American won the heart of Thelma Caplan over the objections of her protective parents who feared, justifiably as it turned out, that she would not be as secure under his roof as she had been under theirs.

As a boy, Frank often spent weekends at his grandparents' house, the site of formative experiences that have become staples of the Gehry legend. First, there was the famous carp bought live each week by his grandmother, an affectionate, devout, hard-working woman who wore a traditional Orthodox wig, and journeyed to and fro between home and

Kensington Market up to three times a day. The fish would live in the bathtub until she killed it on Friday to make gefilte fish for the Sabbath. When Gehry began to use the fish motif in his designs in the 1980s, he took to evoking the primal carp.

Baba, as her grandchildren called her, was the neighbourhood healer and herbalist. Shirley Solway, Frank's first cousin who also spent the better part of her childhood at the house, recalls: "There were always strangers at the kitchen table" seeking her remedies. Her grandchildren adored her. "My grandmother used to get the wood for her stove from a wood shop on Sullivan Street," Gehry recounts. "She would take a burlap bag full of cuttings, and she'd spill them out on the floor. Then, we would make cities." Years later, he would come to understand this activity as sympathetic to his own intuitive process, as a kind of licence for an adult to play. Wood itself – used notably in Gehry's bentwood chairs, which he has linked to the bushel baskets he played with as a child – features prominently in recent designs, including the AGO and his own new house in Venice, California. Says Gehry: "I find a comfort in wood. It's something I feel good with."

His grandfather, with whom he read the Talmud and recited morning prayers, was president of his local synagogue, the Talmud Torah on D'Arcy Street, where Frank had his bar mitzvah. Sam Caplan

tempered orthodoxy with business sense; he would get his grandson to keep the hardware store open on Saturday morning while he attended shul. Frank helped out at the store after school and on weekends. He relished working with his hands, and with the raw building materials that later became important to his architectural aesthetic. "That nurtured it: learning to work with pipe, to cut pipe, put the threads on it, to cut glass, sell putty, sell nails, sell bolts," he reminisces, laughing softly. "I used to love opening those boxes of bolts and looking at them, and making stuff with them. I loved all that."

Poor by today's standards, the Caplans were well off by comparison with the newer immigrant families crowded into nearby tenements and with the growing ranks of beggars in the streets in the wake of the Depression. By 1934, the year Toronto celebrated its centenary with lavish fireworks on Toronto Island, there were 120,000 men on relief. Hard times accentuated the values of hard work and self-sacrifice held by families such as the Caplans. None of the large tribe of cousins, with whom young Frank played in back alleys and attended 25-cent Saturday matinees at Shea's Theatre, enrolled in university until the 1950s.

The Jewish neighbourhood, extending roughly from Queen Street north to Harbord Street and University Avenue east to Grace Street, formed a

kind of extension of family life; it was dotted with synagogues, kosher creameries, tailor shops, delis, chicken markets  where you picked out a live bird to be plucked at home, and a Yiddish cinema on Spadina Avenue, which Frank attended with his grandmother. It was a village whose old-world orthodoxy was evident in the candle-lit darkness that descended every Friday at sundown, and in the flow of families walking to services on Saturday morning.

By contrast with this steady, rooted existence was the more volatile life Frank led with his immediate family (a sister, Doreen, was born in 1931), who lived outside the ghetto proper, around Dundas Street and Rusholme Road. At first the family lived in a series of rented rooms, but by the mid-1930s Irving Goldberg's income from leasing and servicing slot machines, pinball machines and juke boxes was sufficient to enable them to afford a down payment on a modest, two-storey brick house at 1364 Dundas Street West, an event Frank remembers as  "a big deal for the family." When his father prospered, he could be generous, but his volatile moods often darkened the household. "He wasn't the great father figure. He was angry most of the time," Gehry recalls. "He liked to draw, and he always wanted me to sit and draw with him. I didn't get into it. I was scared of him – all I wanted to do was get away."

Irving, who had trained as a boxer, was anti-intellectual and insecure about his lack of formal education. (Frank remembers his father saying to one of his teachers, "I don't know no vocabulary words".) In hindsight, Gehry admires his father's democratic spirit, which stood out in an era of open prejudice and snobbery. "My father was politically open; he brought all kinds of people to the house. He brought in the French-Canadians in Timmins; I remember a blind, black boxer we had as a babysitter." Gehry, too, positions himself as a foe of intellectual pomposity, and as a champion of populist values. As an adult, he took up boxing. A gifted storyteller, he speaks, as one observer has pointed out, like a tough guy from an early Hollywood movie. Although his much-vaunted lack of pretension may in itself constitute a form of pretension, it is a huge part of his charm.

As an architect and designer, Frank Gehry draws on an enviable range of high-to-low cultural references that is, in part, the divergent legacy of his parents. Famed for the rough elegance of his style, he is the only member of his rarified profession to have won its most prestigious prize (the Pritzker in 1989) *and* to have achieved the status of a household name. (He is notably the only architect to have played himself in an episode of *The Simpsons*.)

If Frank absorbed popular culture from his

father, he shifted into high gear with his mother, a warm-hearted woman with whom he enjoyed a lifelong bond. As well as being "uppity and into Hadassah," she was into the arts, and took her children to the Royal Ontario Museum, to Massey Hall and to the Art Gallery of Toronto.

In her confident embrace of the city, Thelma Goldberg differed from more recent immigrants, who tended to shy away from public institutions such as the art museum. She enrolled young Frank in art classes there and marched confidently through its imposing wrought iron gates. "Did I think it was for the goyim? No way," says Gehry. "I went there. My mother took me." He recalls the sight of Sir Ernest MacMillan, then the conductor of the Toronto Symphony, riding on a bicycle through the streets of the city. "On my way to Bloor Collegiate, I would pass the racetrack – which is now a park – and I remember waving to him as he rode by. I knew who he was because we had been to Massey Hall to hear him." Gehry noted that his parents chose to live outside the Jewish ghetto and to send their children to integrated schools. "They didn't think Jewish," he says. "They thought worldly."

That took courage, as Depression-era Toronto was not exactly free of anti-Semitism. The economic downturn prompted Canada to sharply curtail immigration in 1931; special quotas for Jews remained in effect until the end of World War II, with disastrous consequences for Europeans attempting to flee the Holocaust. The professional schools at the University of Toronto also controlled the admission of Jews through quotas. Jews were widely blamed for spreading trade unionism and Communism, and the Toronto police enjoyed frightening discretionary powers to crack down on suspected sedition. Gehry remembers the anxiety at his grandmother's house around secret union meetings held there late at night by her brother, who worked in the garment trade.

Yet Toronto was a haven of tolerance compared to Timmins, where the Goldberg family spent two miserable years from 1940 to 1942. There were about thirty Jewish families in Timmins; Frankie Goldberg was the only Jew at his school, where he was nicknamed Fishhead, implying a bad smell. "I used to go out at recess to play hockey and I'd get beat up. The French-Canadians from the school next door shared the same rink, and they used to stand up for me." The Goldbergs were closer to the Jewish community in Timmins than they had been in Toronto: "You clung together for support because there was a bloody wall of anti-Semitism outside."

In 1942, when the family left Timmins suddenly as a result of a government ban on slot machines, Frank was happy to get out. His father, however, would never recover from the loss of livelihood. "Back in Toronto, my father started a new business – it was just stupid, making things like wooden trays, smoking stands, lazy susans," recalls Gehry for whom the memory is still visibly painful. "Sometimes, I worked with him. It makes me cry, with what I know now, to think how I could have helped him. We could have had fun together." The venture collapsed, and his father's health and morale with it. Within a few years, the Goldbergs had sold the house on Dundas Street, and squeezed in with the grandparents on Beverley, where a set of down-on-their-luck cousins were already ensconced. In all, they were ten, sharing a single bathroom.

Later in life, Gehry opined that the ordeal of anti-Semitism might have been useful in a spine-stiffening sort of way. Yet rejection and financial failure left their mark. No matter how successful he is, at some inner level, he is always walking on thin ice. "Always the outsider," is the way he describes himself, "because of the family, and because of the Jewish thing in Timmins. I think that gets built into you – that you're the outsider."

Still, the rebellious risk taker who would one day revolutionize architecture was not apparent in adolescence. A so-so student at Bloor Collegiate, a small, academically oriented high school at Bloor and Dufferin, he liked to draw and to make things in the shop course. Too short for football, he became a cheerleader instead. He had a best friend, Ross Honsberger, with whom he played ping-pong and handball at the West End YMCA, and he belonged to a twelve-member Jewish fraternity, which met on weekends. He enjoyed a minor reputation for radicalism when he and Ross tried briefly to convert other students to their newly found philosophy of atheism. Other than that, he was, by all accounts, unremarkable, a short, pudgy, black-haired boy who was happy just to fit in. Friendly and well liked, he gave no outward sign of his increasingly troubled home life or of a destiny beyond the average.

Only his mother singled him out for greatness. "My father thought I was a dreamer, I wasn't going to amount to anything. My mother thought I was just reticent to do things. She would push me," he told *Time* magazine in 2001. It was Thelma who arranged to have his handwriting analyzed, and who made "a big deal" of the analyst's conclusion that he would one day become a famous architect. It was Thelma who was "always talking" about a firm of Jewish architects in Toronto. She, herself, later became "legendary" as an interior designer at a posh Los Angeles department store; one of his father's sisters also made a name for herself as a dress designer in Miami. "The creativity was there in the family genes," he notes, "but we were so poor and fucked-up we didn't know what to do with it."

Spurred on by his mother, Gehry pondered architecture in a desultory way. At a lecture series at the University of Toronto ("I realize in hindsight it was kind of rare for a sixteen-year-old to spend his Friday nights going to lectures," he muses), he heard the great Finnish architect Alvar Aalto speak and present his 1931 Paimio chair, a curved and moulded birchwood piece that anticipated Gehry's own later creations. In vocational guidance at Bloor Collegiate, he researched the architectural program at the University of Toronto, which was then stodgy in the extreme. He recalls losing interest, "because it looked so bloody boring." Gehry has always maintained that he would never have become an architect had he remained in Canada.

By Frank's last year at Bloor Collegiate, the crisis at home made hopes for the future seem irrelevant. After a doctor advised that Irving's health might improve in a warmer climate, they decided to take the drastic step of moving to Los Angeles, where two of his brothers were living. "It was a sacrifice for my mother to leave. Her mother was a big deal for her. It was a sacrifice for me. I had my friends – I loved it here." He did not complete high school because of the stress: "My father's problems got so much in the way toward the end. It was desperate. As the man in the family, it was my job to go to work. I thought I was never going to college. There was no future."

Frank Gehry did not return to Toronto until 1962, when he, his first wife and two daughters passed through on their way back to Los Angeles after a year in Paris. By then, Frankie Goldberg, ordinary Canadian, had become Frank Gehry, American architect,[2] following the classic plot lines of the American dream. "For a long time, I couldn't go back," he says. "We had no money and it was so painful out here getting going. I had dual citizenship because my father was an American. At the age of twenty-one, I had to choose. By then, I identified with L.A."

History has a way of looping back on itself. In Gehry's case, it took half a century. In 2002, the year he finally got the chance to put his stamp on a major cultural institution in Canada with the AGO project, then-Prime Minister Jean Chrétien gave him back his long-lost dual citizenship. "I love Canada," says Gehry, who now uses his Canadian passport to travel outside the U.S. "I'm happy to be a citizen again. Politically, I relate more to it."

Frank Gehry's roots in Canada are deep and wide. From the original family of Polish immigrants, he has over two hundred relatives in the Toronto region, many of whom probably don't know they are related to him, says his cousin Elinor Caplan, the former Liberal cabinet minister and MP for Thornhill. When Gehry unveiled his AGO design in January, 2004, the core group of relatives with whom he had stayed in touch over the years were there. "We feel very warmly toward him," says Shirley Solway. "He was always darling, always sweet. He is the same old Frank, except that now he drops names that everyone knows."

The boy who once listened enraptured to Foster Hewitt on Saturday night radio now hangs out with hockey's legendary heroes. "Did you know I just had dinner the other night with Red Kelly at Frank Mahovlich's house?" he asks, chuckling in amazement. The boy who once waved at Sir Ernest MacMillan now designs international concert halls and befriends the world's leading musicians. The boy who once stood wide-eyed in Walker Court now watches closely as his vision for the Art Gallery of Ontario takes shape for a new generation. ■

**Endnotes**

1    In 1954 Frank changed his name from Goldberg to Gehry at the request of his first wife, Anita. The change made sense to him at the time, given the prevailing climate of anti-Semitism, but Gehry has often expressed regret about it since. His first marriage (which produced two daughters, Leslie and Brina) ended in 1966. He married Berta Aguilera in 1975, and the couple has two sons, Alejandro and Sam.

2    Gehry received his Bachelor of Architecture from the University of Southern California in 1954, having put himself through school with a truck-driving job and with help from his first wife. In 1956–57 he studied city planning at the Harvard Graduate School of Design, but quit in frustration at the tedium of the process. He worked with different architects before opening his first L.A. office in 1962.

Although he had left Toronto with his family for Los Angeles in 1947 when he was eighteen years old, Gehry still had strong feelings for the city, and particularly the neighbourhood of Grange Park.

ART GALLERY OF TORONTO

# A Century of Building the Art Gallery of Ontario

Dennis Reid

When *Transformation AGO* was officially announced late in 2002, the challenge presented to the chosen architect, Frank Gehry, was to not only provide imaginative new spaces for the renowned Thomson Collection on an already full site, but essentially to re-think how the entire building could best serve the institution it housed as it entered its second century. It is a complex building, an accretion of parts, each added in response to the perceived needs of its time and always, it would seem, with an eye to posterity. Each succeeding design also has responded in some fashion to the historical structure of the building, some in ways that disappoint, and others with real success, but none as brilliantly as that of Frank Gehry.

Eighteen years elapsed after the establishment in 1900 of the Art Museum of Toronto before its first purpose-built galleries were opened, and then just about a twentieth of the planned space was realized. Founded by a group of interested artists, collectors and civic leaders, the fledgling museum made its first purchase of a work of art only in 1909, and organized but three loan exhibitions during its initial decade. Its first big boost came in 1910 when it was publicly announced that Harriette Boulton Smith had left her historic home, The Grange, and its seven acres of property to the art museum (fig. 1). The following year the museum concluded an agreement with the city to make available the bulk of the property, that portion south of The Grange, as a public park, with the understanding that the city would expropriate the house lots along then St. Patrick (now Dundas) Street to allow for the expansion of the museum to the north. The acquisition of these properties, which had begun in 1910, was completed in 1914 (although not all the houses were actually cleared away until 1924).

The 1911 agreement with the city nonetheless allowed the art museum's board to begin planning for a building to augment The Grange. That same year, under the leadership of their president, Sir Edmund Walker, the board engaged the prominent Toronto architecture firm Darling & Pearson, who the following year would undertake the design of the first wing of the Royal Ontario Museum (completed 1914), where Walker also headed the board. Frank Darling, lead architect, submitted his initial plans in 1912, the year the art museum first occupied The Grange. Further plans and estimates were submitted in 1914, but these were considered too expensive and were modified. Then all fundraising and further planning was halted because of WW I. In 1916, however, the board decided to go ahead with a small section of the approved plan, and construction commenced that October. The grand beaux-arts scheme consisted of some thirty galleries organized around three open interior courtyards,

a total of approximately 83,250 square feet (7,734 square metres). To be built in stone and facing Dundas Street, the building would comfortably have occupied much of the land north of The Grange between Beverley and McCaul streets (fig. 2). What actually opened in April 1918 was the middle (and smallest) of the planned three large south galleries, the one closest to The Grange (fig. 3). Known as the Long Gallery, it had a small square gallery to the east and a small octagon gallery to the west, comprising altogether about 7,000 square feet (650 square metres). Finished in stone on the exterior, it was connected to The Grange by a corridor. A year later another corridor was run north to establish a new main entrance off Dundas Street.

Eight more years passed before a subsequent stage of the Darling & Pearson scheme was realized, and that too was in a truncated form. About one half of the planned central sculpture court north of the Long Gallery was completed, although as an indoor space, not open as in the original plan, and with a gallery and rotunda on either side and a small print room on the second floor over a new central entrance on Dundas Street (fig. 3). When it opened in January 1926, the sculpture court was named the Sir Edmund Walker Memorial Court after the principal founder and first president of the art museum, or the Art Gallery of Toronto, as it had been renamed

Fig.1

in 1919. In 1933 a doorway was cut into the Long Gallery in-line with the central axis of Walker Court and the front entrance on Dundas Street. Then in 1935 two more small galleries, designed by Darling, Pearson & Cleveland Architects, were added on either side of the Dundas Street elevation (figs. 3 and 4), but after that there was no new construction for thirty-five years.

In response to its growing collections and a sense of a larger role for the institution both locally and internationally, the Gallery again began to plan expansion in 1968, just at the end of Samuel Zacks's term as president. The collections had been growing steadily on all fronts over the previous thirty-five years, but it was the promise of a gift from renowned

British sculptor Henry Moore of forty of his major plasters, twelve bronzes, a large selection of drawings and maquettes, and an almost complete set of his prints that was the catalyst, and also the prospect of the famous Zacks collection of modern European and Canadian paintings and sculptures. In addition, the Gallery had mounted a series of international loan exhibitions during the mid-1960s (when Samuel Zacks was chairman of the exhibition committee) of unprecedented ambition – major retrospectives devoted to Canaletto, Eugène Delacroix, Pablo Picasso and Piet Mondrian – and had to dismantle the permanent collection displays every time to accommodate them. Probably even more importantly, in 1966 the Gallery had entered into a partnership with the Province of Ontario to deliver an expanded education program and a circulating exhibition program throughout the province; the same year it was renamed the Art Gallery of Ontario to reflect this larger mandate.

There was, not surprisingly, little if any thought given to completing the Darling & Pearson master plan. Needs had changed dramatically. The board of the Gallery did, however, turn again to the most prominent Toronto architect of the day, John C. Parkin, whose reputation rested on a number of high profile modernist buildings, including Terminal 1 at Toronto International Airport (1964). Again not surprisingly, this time they

decided from the outset to phase the completion of
their ambitious plans over three stages. Construction
of the first stage, an expansion to the north and east
of the Darling & Pearson building, began in 1971 and
was completed in October 1974. Most of the interior
of the original structure was preserved inside Parkin's
building, which extended north virtually to the extent
proposed by the original, unrealized Darling & Pearson
scheme. A prominent feature was a sunken driveway
that allowed cars from Dundas Street down to drop
off passengers at a lower lobby, providing access to
education and extension offices at that level, as well
as from there to the main lobby via a large, open double
stairway up to the first floor (fig. 5). Further east along
Dundas at the lower level was a fully equipped, raked-
seating theatre with its own entrance off McCaul Street.

The main entrance from Dundas Street to the
first-floor upper lobby was across a wide bridge over
the sunken drive (fig. 6). Inside, a split stairway led
down to the lower level on either side of another bridge,
which led on the upper level through a glass wall
that separated the lobby area from the more carefully
acclimatized part of the building directly into a new
gallery space just north of Walker Court, and thence
into all the original Darling & Pearson galleries (fig. 7).

The modern pre-cast concrete structure contained
a range of new facilities including the Henry Moore

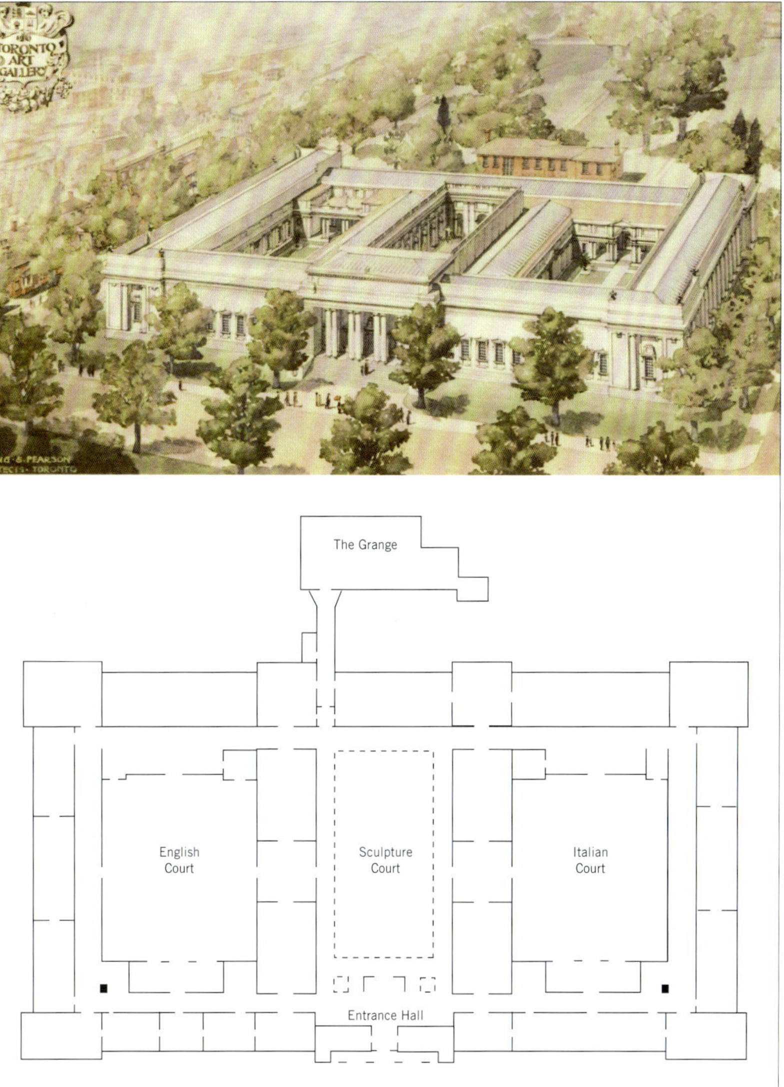


Fig. 2

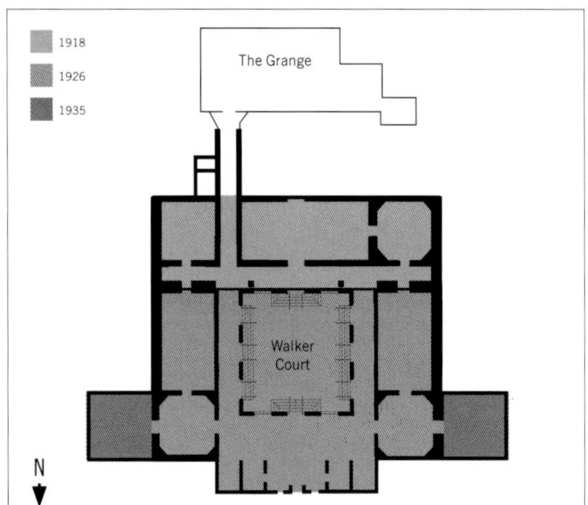

Fig. 3

Darling & Pearson built program, 1918–1935

Dundas Street façade of the completed Darling, Pearson & Cleveland building.

Collection of the Edward P. Taylor Research Library and Archives, AGO

Fig.4

Sculpture Centre, a new contemporary art space, the Sam and Ayala Zacks Pavilion for temporary exhibitions, and a new Gallery Shop. As well as public space, Stage I established a range of professional museum facilities, including a state-of-the-art conservation studio, storage vaults, exhibition preparation shops, a photographic studio and administrative offices. The Grange, freed from sixty years of service as administrative offices and library, was lovingly restored by preservation architect Peter Stokes and historical consultant Jeanne Minhinnick to reflect upper-class domestic life in nineteenth-century Toronto.

Construction of Stage II commenced shortly after the opening of Stage I, and it was completed three years later, opening in September 1977 (fig. 5). A new west wing along Beverley Street provided further education and extension facilities, a new audio-visual library, a new space for the reference library and a new small gallery. On the second floor, the new wing featured a large gallery space for contemporary art called the Signy Eaton Gallery and a three-gallery suite dedicated to the Canadian historical collection.

Stage III of the Parkin grand plan initially called for an extension south beyond The Grange into Grange Park (fig. 8), but public opposition led to the decision that the addition would extend only as far as the back

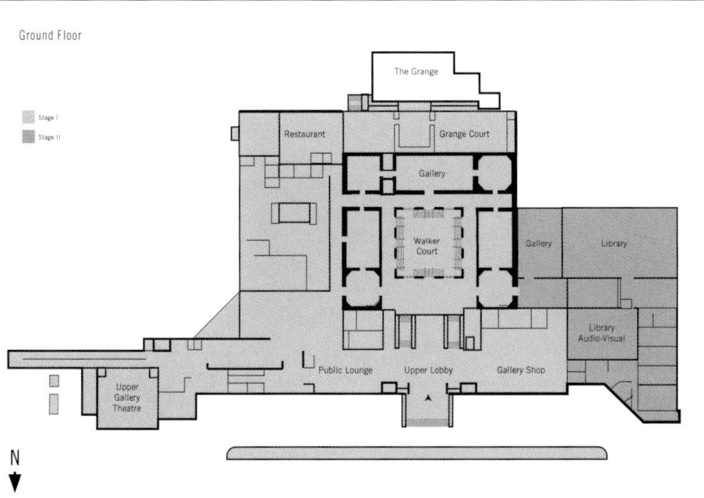


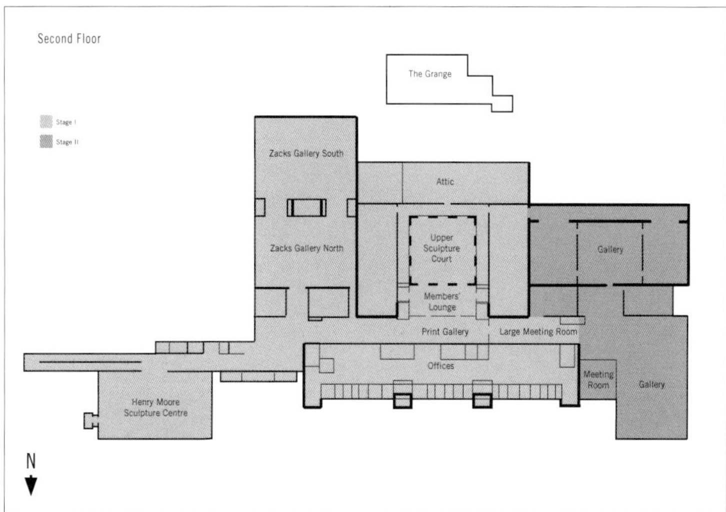


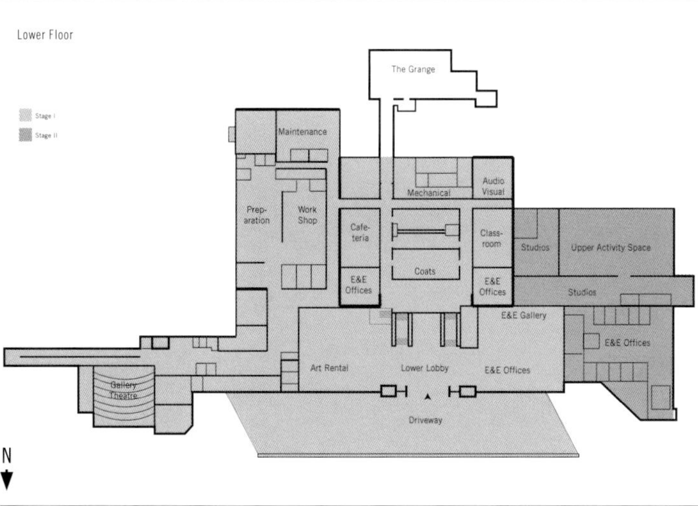


Fig. 5 Parkin-built, program, Stages I and II

Fig. 6 The main entrance, 1974
Collection of the Edward P. Taylor Research Library and Archives, AGO

Fig.7

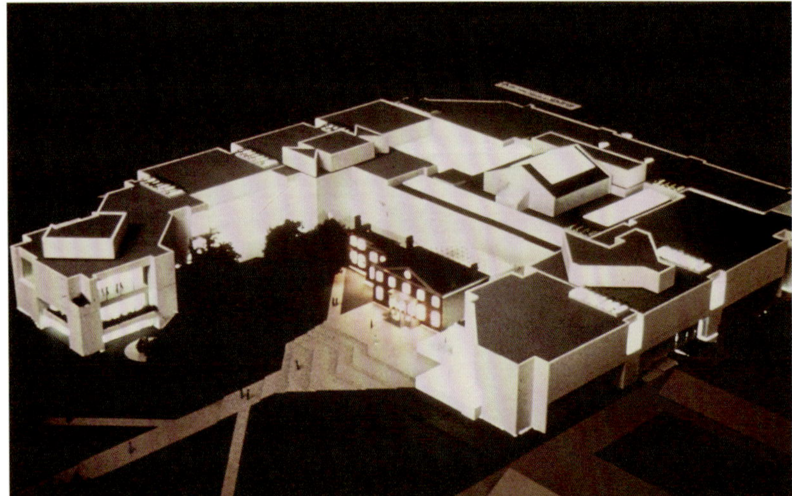

Fig.8

wall of The Grange. Construction was delayed for lack of funds, however, and, when planning resumed in 1982, the needs of the program inevitably had increased. A decision was made this time to choose an architect through competition. By the time it was launched in the summer of 1986, the project was expected to increase gallery space by fifty percent to display the contemporary, Inuit and sculpture collections, and to provide a print and drawing centre, a vault for works on paper, a new library, increased space for technical workshops and conservation studios, more retail space, and improved public accessibility and circulation. In 1987 the Stage III project was awarded to Barton Myers Architects Inc., whose principal, Barton Myers, had been based in Toronto since 1968. He had relocated to Los Angeles in 1987, however, and so for the purposes of the project entered into a joint venture with the local firm Kuwabara Payne McKenna Blumberg, a young practice formed by his former senior associates in Toronto. Construction commenced in the fall of 1989 and was completed in January 1993 (fig. 9).

While retaining Parkin's pre-cast concrete Moore Centre to the east and the Signy Eaton Gallery to the western extremity, Myers/KPMB rethought entirely the Dundas Street elevation in between. They filled in the moat-like drive that led to the lower entrance, creating a long, narrow, slightly elevated terrace along Dundas

Street and a platform for a new brick structure that rose two storeys, capped with a metal barrel-vaulted roof (fig. 10). Most dramatically they moved the main entrance further east, just west of the Moore Centre, which allowed them to create a soaring, three-storey-high, open lobby space beneath a striking pyramidal roof. The lobby led visitors up a short flight of stairs, through a glass wall and directly into a long, narrow gallery, one of a linked series of spaces that somewhat awkwardly formed an east-west corridor, which acted as the main access to galleries on the first and second floors. The first floor also included an expanded Gallery Shop. The lower level was entirely turned over to education facilities, including a new small lecture theatre and a "hands-on" space for children. On the second floor, what had been office space along Dundas Street was turned into contemporary galleries, distinguished by a soaring barrel vaulted roof. The old boardroom became a dedicated space for Inuit art.

The administrative offices dislodged from Dundas Street were relocated in a compact four-storey addition to the southwest corner, called the Chalmers Wing. The first floor of this new wing was taken up entirely by an elegant print and drawing study centre overlooking Grange Park. Beneath this facility on the lower level was an equally elegant research library and archive, with a similarly fine reading room and adjacent stacks to the north. New print and drawing galleries connected to another architectural highlight of Stage III, the Joey and Toby Tanenbaum Sculpture Atrium, a soaring glass-and-steel structure that connected the Chalmers Wing to the Zacks Pavilion, and The Grange to the original 1918 Darling & Pearson façade.

Within three years of the completion of Stage III, the Gallery began again actively planning for expansion. The catalyst this time was the prospect of the donation of Kenneth Thomson's remarkable personal collection, at first the Canadian works, but soon also the European pieces. One of the finest collections of small sculptures and other rare art objects dating from the twelfth to the nineteenth centuries, it will transform how the AGO is perceived internationally. A clear path forward was not initially evident (it was particularly difficult to imagine significant expansion on what was an already full site), and discussions laboured on for another three years. Then it was decided to bring Toronto-born, internationally renowned architect Frank Gehry into the mix, and an initial meeting was held with him in the spring of 2000. Government and community leadership support was secured over the next two and a half years, and in November 2002 the *Transformation AGO* project was launched with the public announcement of Kenneth Thomson's gift of his collection along with a large cash donation toward realizing an

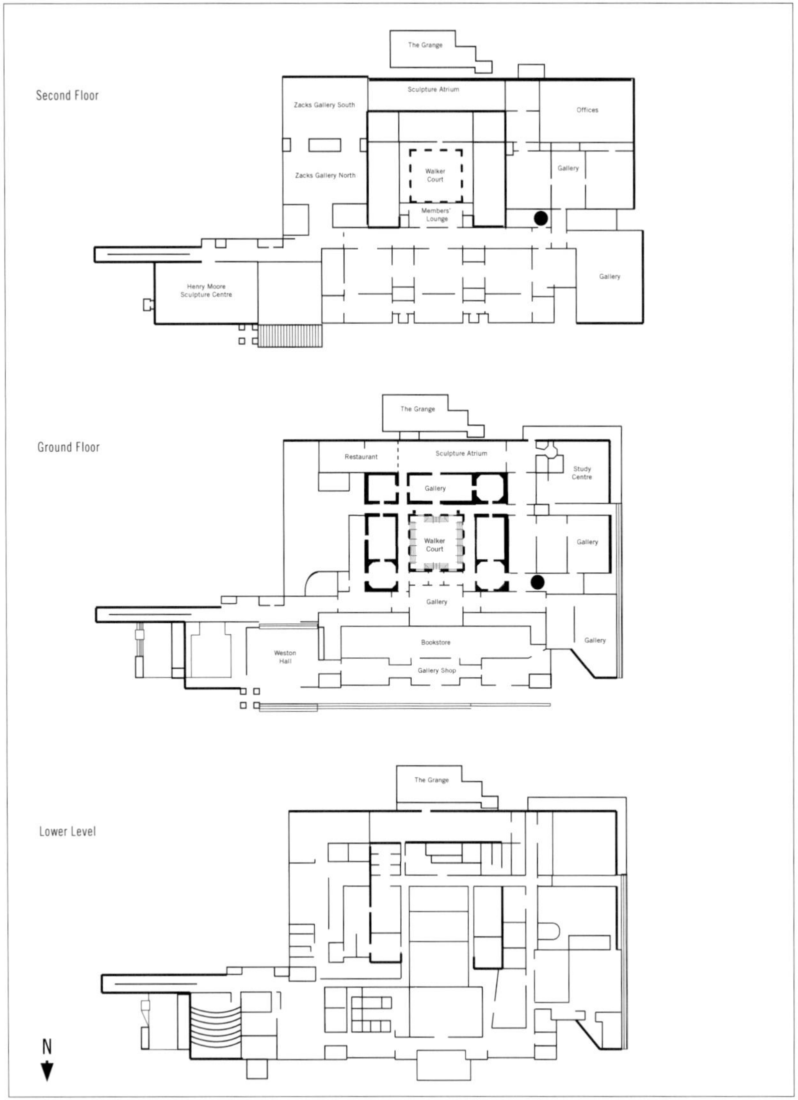

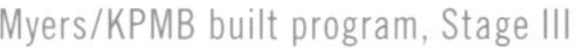

Fig.9

Myers/KPMB built program, Stage III

expanded facility to be designed by Frank Gehry.

Although he had left Toronto with his family for Los Angeles in 1947 when he was eighteen years old, Gehry still had strong feelings for the city and particularly the neighbourhood of Grange Park. His grandmother had lived just south of the park on Beverley Street, and he had often played under its trees as a child. His first affecting experience of art was in the Art Gallery of Toronto, one that was inextricably entwined with the memory of Walker Court. It is not surprising then that as planning discussions began, Gehry's first, almost instinctive, move was to realign the front entrance and lobby with Walker Court. His respect for the court and for the Grange Park neighbourhood was the single constant throughout his freely creative initial stages of design. Among the range of ideas explored were towers of different conformation along Dundas Street and a large new structure of various shapes over the original 1918 Darling & Pearson structure and sculpture atrium on the south side. His schematic design proposal was unveiled in January 2004 and the final plan was confirmed that fall (fig. 11). Construction began in June 2005 with completion expected in mid-2008.

Gehry, like Myers/KPMB, decided to retain the Parkin pre-cast concrete Dundas Street "bookends" of the Henry Moore Sculpture Centre and Signy

Eaton Gallery, and also like Myers/KPMB, to rework entirely the space in between. Parkin had placed the Gallery Shop along Dundas Street to allow him to open up windows to the street, although any real sense of accessibility this presented was undercut by the "moat" that separated the building from the thoroughfare. Myers/KPMB brought the façade closer to the street and extended the shop behind huge windows almost the whole length of the block, but they were unable to deal with the grade change between the Gallery's first floor and the sidewalk other than by creating a terrace with steps down to the street. The large, welcoming canopy that marked their new entrance and lobby helped, and a planned, but never completed, smaller canopy that was to extend the whole length of the terrace to the west might have helped more, but finally the Myers/KPMB-designed AGO still retained an aloof distance from the street.

Gehry's bold design promises a breakthrough. Most dramatically he has created a great glass cowl over a Douglas fir frame that extends right across the Dundas Street façade and rises over two storeys high to enclose a grand sculpture promenade on the second floor that promises views to and from the city. This cowl swoops down over the sidewalk almost to the curb, effectively forming a protective canopy the entire length of the structure (fig. 12).

Fig.10

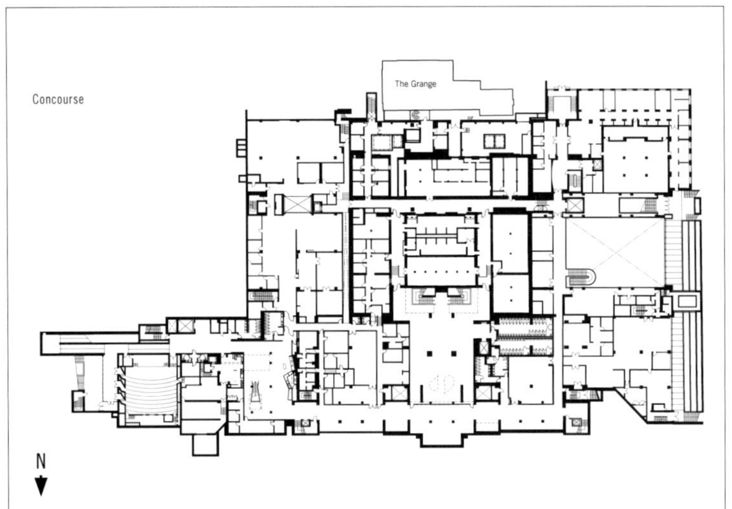


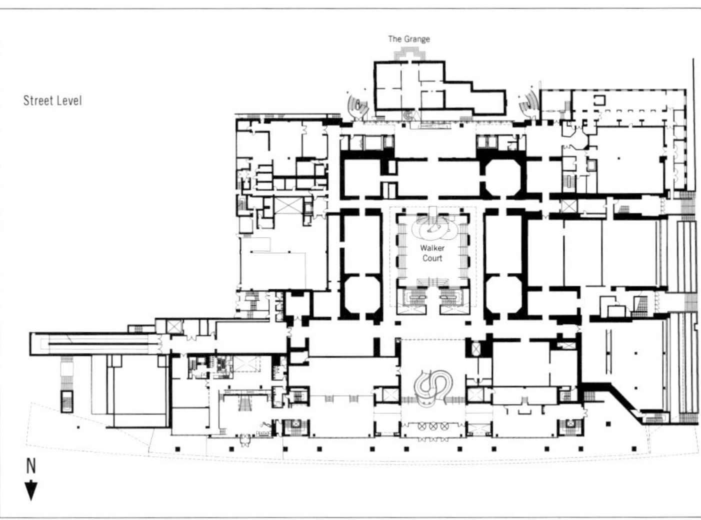


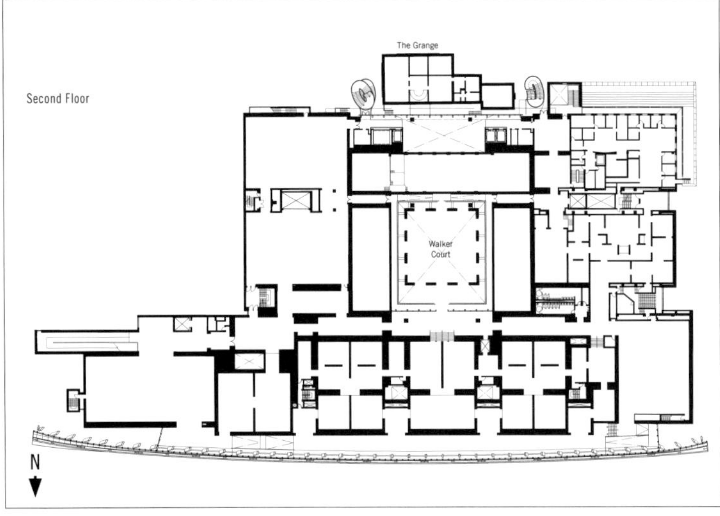


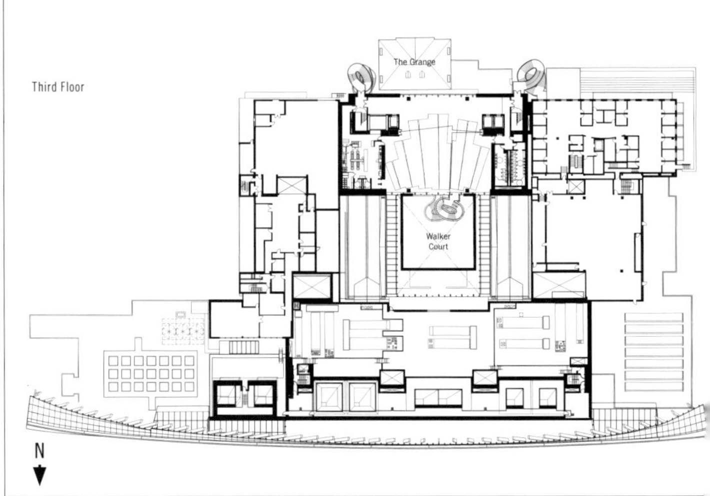


Fig.11 Gehry floor plans and site plan
Courtesy of Gehry Partners, LLP

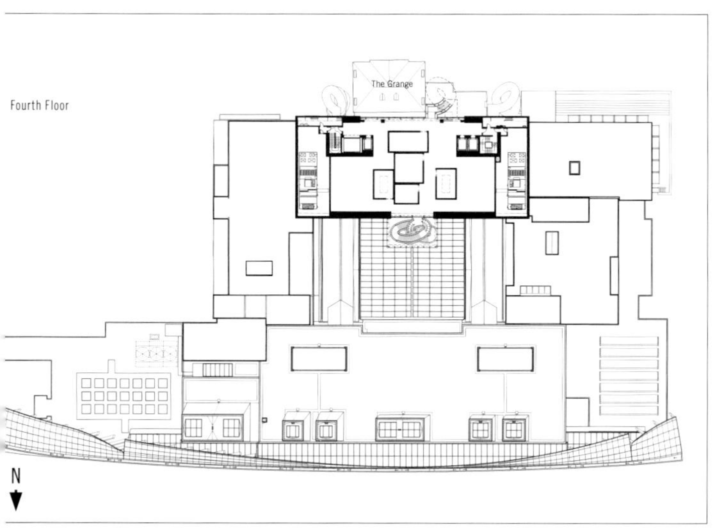


Fourth Floor
The Grange
N


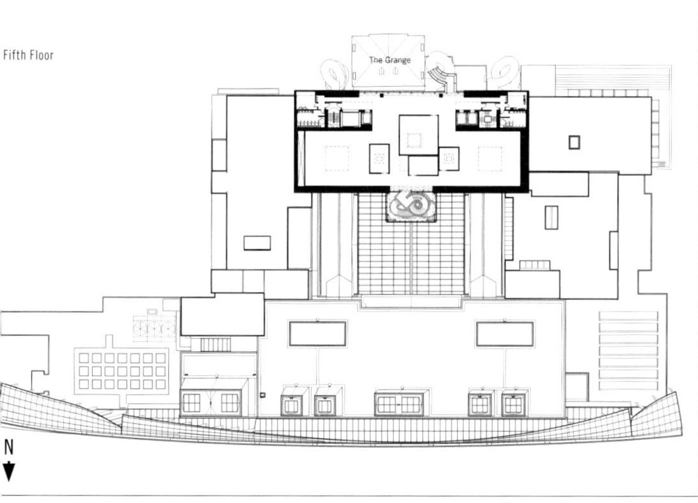


Fifth Floor
The Grange
N


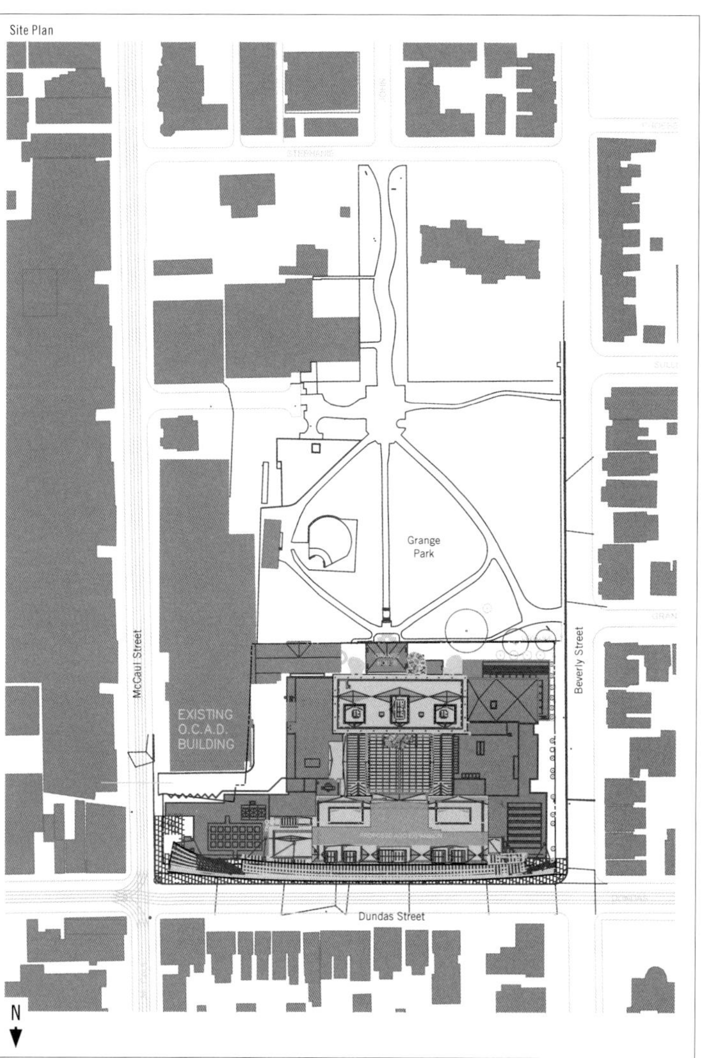


Site Plan
Grange
Park
McCaul Street
Beverly Street
EXISTING
O.C.A.D.
BUILDING
Dundas Street
N

Fig.12

Fig.13



Gehry's other significant initiative and guiding design principle is to realign the main entrance to the centrally located Walker Court, as it was in the original Darling & Pearson and the Parkin buildings. After traversing a coiled ramp of Douglas fir (one of Gehry's signature elements) just inside the entrance, the visitor will experience an unobstructed view through Walker Court and into the original 1918 building, and on into the Joey and Tobey Tanenbaum Sculpture Atrium and The Grange: a clear line, literally, right through the building from Dundas Street to Grange Park. The centrality of Walker Court to this new vision of the Gallery will be emphasized by giving it a new glass roof that will fill it with natural light. A new scissor stairway of Douglas fir leads up to the second floor and down through an open well to the renewed lower level, creating in its midst a dynamic reminiscence of Parkin's "bridge" from the lobby into Walker Court. Catwalks tucked up under the second-floor arcades on either side of Walker Court meet on the south side at another spectacular Douglas fir staircase that will twist out through the top of the court, through the glass roof, and spiral up to connect with three new floors to the south. Standing in Walker Court visitors will be able to see their way to virtually every destination in the building.

By repositioning Walker Court as the centre of a new strong north-south axis and as the principal point for vertical movement, Gehry has taken pressure off the single east-west corridor concept that proved so problematic for Myers/KPMB. On the first floor these quasi-corridor spaces will relax into real gallery spaces directly accessible from Walker Court: along the east into the brilliantly reconfigured spaces that will house the Thomson European collection or along the west into new spaces for early twentieth-century European art and the photography and prints and drawings suite of galleries. On the second floor at the landing, the choices will be equally clear: the Thomson Canadian collection straight ahead, the rest of the Canadian wing left to the west, and to the east the Zacks Pavilion for special exhibitions, a new gallery for African and Oceanic art, and the Henry Moore Sculpture Centre. On the north side of the Thomson Canadian galleries, the sculpture promenade will connect through new doorways with the Signy Eaton Gallery at the west end and the Moore centre at the east, and offer access as well through five points into the Thomson galleries in between.

The new construction to the south will rise three storeys above the original 1918 building and the sculpture atrium – a big box shape clad in titanium that will house a hosting centre on its lower floor and a new centre for contemporary art on the upper two floors. Windows to the south will provide spectacular views of Grange Park and the city beyond, while the view of the south face of the new AGO from the city will be equally satisfying. Of particular note is the positioning of a spiral staircase that pops out of the south face of the building to connect the top two floors of contemporary galleries (fig. 13). That staircase and two more staircases, fire exits that coil gently down on either side of The Grange, establish a respectful tension with that first home of the Gallery, showcasing it brilliantly against the huge, seemingly always evolving institution to which it first gave substantial form. ∎

New architectural energy will radiate from the historic core, opening the institution to the city and the city to the institution.

Fig. I

# Frank Gehry:
# Seeing the AGO Again (and Again)

Old paint on canvas, as it ages, sometimes
becomes transparent. When that happens it is
possible, in some pictures, to see the original
lines: a tree will show through a woman's dress,
a child makes way for a dog, a large boat is no
longer on an open sea. That is called pentimento
because the painter "repented," changed his
mind. Perhaps it would be as well to say that
the old conception, replaced by a later choice,
is a way of seeing and then seeing again.
— Lillian Hellman

Larry Wayne Richards

Near the beginning of Gehry Partners's drawings
for the Art Gallery of Ontario, there is a sheet titled
"Site Geometry Plan." In the centre one finds a small
dimensioned plan of the AGO's 1926 Walker Court with
a north-south dotted line running through it. The line
leads to a text at the bottom of the page that states,
"The centre line of Walker Court is an organizing element
of the project geometry and dimensioning"(fig. 2).[1]

Although this technical directive might at first seem
relatively unimportant to the grand transformation of
the AGO, it takes on significance when Frank Gehry
recalls his first visit to the museum with his mother,
Thelma Goldberg, during his Toronto youth: "It was
my first time in an art museum. I think I was eight years
old, and my mother took me. There was snow on the
ground, and we were wearing galoshes. I remember
a fence and a driveway and iron gates. The building
was set back from the street, and you walked right
into Walker Court."[2] Continuing his focus on Walker
Court, Gehry notes that "when the AGO hired me
I saw right away that the circulation had become
confusing. The original building had been added to
piecemeal. My sense was, if we were going to redo
the AGO, you could solve the confusion by centering
the main entrance on the historic Walker Court."[3]

History comes full circle in the coincidence of
Gehry's personal memory of the AGO, his sense that the

main entrance had to be re-centred on Walker Court, and his office's establishment of the centre line of the court as the primary organizing element for the project's technical drawings. The revitalized Walker Court, with its remarkable new staircase (fig. 1), can be seen as the epicentre of Frank Gehry's design for the Art Gallery of Ontario. New architectural energy will radiate from the historic core, opening the institution to the city and the city to the institution.

Moreover, in assessing the transformation of the AGO, it is possible to imagine a sphere of deployment – one that, in the shadows of Cubism, cuts, layers, slices and explodes. The resulting architecture will enable visitors to see and experience the AGO buildings and art in surprising new ways. Gehry treats the place as a grand village that will now step upward and stretch outward. A north-south cross-section from Dundas Street West through Walker Court and The Grange house to Grange Park, reveals both the dynamism and the village-like, spatial intricacy (fig. 3).

At a civic scale, the AGO will seem to reach far beyond its real boundaries. Its boldest new element, a 600-foot-long (183 m), concave-convex canopy and second-level sculpture promenade stretching along Dundas Street (fig. 4), will embrace the everyday activity of the street,

**NOTE REGARDING GEOMETRIC CONSTRUCTION OF WALKER COURT CENTERLINE:**

THE CENTERLINE OF WALKER COURT IS AN ORGANIZING ELEMENT OF THE PROJECT GEOMETRY AND DIMENSIONING. THIS CENTERLINE IS ESTABLISHED ON THE GROUND FLOOR AND TRANSLATES VERTICALLY TO UPPER AND LOWER FLOORS.

THE CENTERLINE IS ESTABLISHED AS FOLLOWS:

1. ESTABLISH POINT 'A' AND 'B' AS THE MIDPOINT SPAN OF THE CENTRAL ARCH ON NORTH AND SOUTH WALL OF WALKER COURT.

2. ESTABLISH POINT 'C' AS THE MIDPOINT BETWEEN POINTS 'A' AND 'B'.

3. ESTABLISH THE 'CENTERLINE OF WALKER COURT' AS THE VECTOR PERPENDICULAR TO THE 'Y–0' GRIDLINE AND PASSING THROUGH POINT 'C'.

Fig. 2

Page 37: Architectural model of new spiral staircase in Walker Court, December 2003

Note from technical drawings for the AGO, August 2005

Transverse section from Dundas Street West to Grange Park, looking east

Courtesy of Gehry Partners, LLP

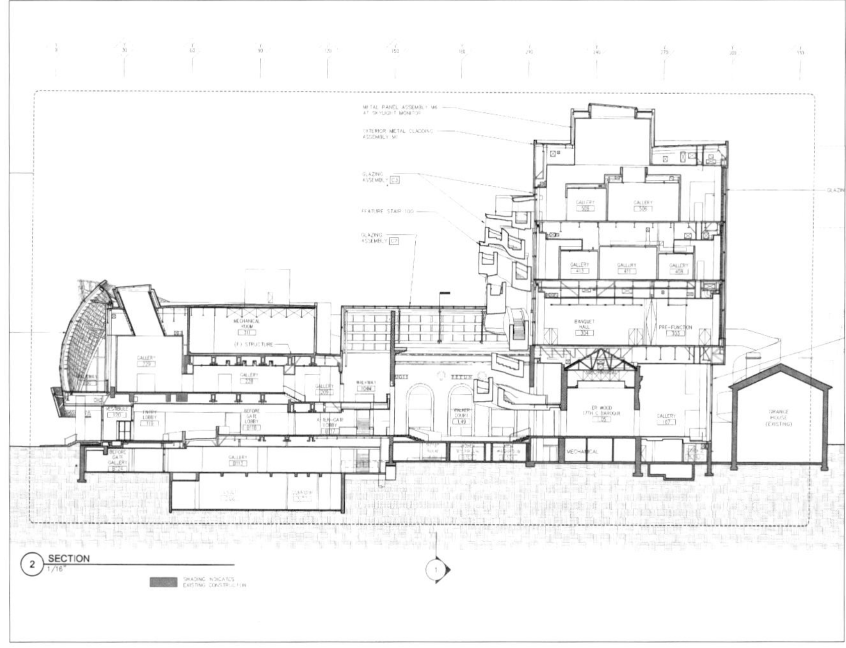

Fig. 3

Fig. 4

Fig. 5

enfolding it into the world of art. A sky-blue volume rising on the south, along with the hovering, Will Alsop-designed Sharp Centre for Design of the Ontario College of Art and Design to the east, will assertively frame and define the urban space of Grange Park.[4]

Within this sphere of architectural action, there will be zoomorphic inhabitants: the astonishing staircase spiralling up from Walker Court, three other unique stairs, and a winding lobby ramp. This family of sculptural insertions reminds us of cirripedes, snakes and worms. (Gehry's staff lovingly named the clinging, external south stairs "the barnacle.") These animal-like forms, along with the sweeping, fish-skeleton volume along Dundas Street, connect to some of Frank Gehry's earliest zoomorphic impulses.

If dynamic village-making and the family of zoomorphic insertions might together be seen as Gehry's two primary architectural strategies, a third permeates both: the opening up and intensifying of conversations between the old and new parts of the buildings – something that Gehry has done with remarkable originality on various projects for forty years. He has a particular way of peeling back the old and layering on the new to create veils of history and to unleash a multiplicity of social experience. Gehry's sometimes subtle, sometimes shocking exposure of the old, then new, then old again, has become highly accomplished and will be one of his gifts to the Art Gallery of Ontario and Toronto.

**Dynamic Extensions**

The possibility of "breaking down the walls" of the Gallery and connecting more aggressively with the city and the public was first signalled in a project by the Montreal-based architect-artist Melvin Charney, installed in the spring of 1978. Titled *Streetwork*, Charney's site-specific installation was part of his exhibition *Other Monuments, 1970–77*."[5] *Streetwork,* was a wood construction, 109 feet in length and 10 feet high that extended through the AGO and outside to Dundas Street. The abstract, inside-to-outside construction underscored Charney's ongoing democratizing agenda, his "attempt to make architecture a less oppressive, more vital element in human affairs."[6] A central question for Charney in the

1970s was: "Where is the dividing line between art and life?" – a question that also preoccupies Frank Gehry.[7]

One of Charney's drawings for *Streetwork* shows his wood construction marching diagonally through the Gallery as a series of rectilinear boxes, then seeming to pierce the wall of the building before reappearing outdoors as a skeletal frame (fig. 5). Informed and developed through Charney's knowledge of Russian Constructivism, *Streetwork*, although modest in comparison, can be seen as a brilliant forerunner of Gehry's Dundas Street intervention some twenty-eight years later. Both projects break down institutional walls, both expose and celebrate wood construction, and both attempt to make architecture a less oppressive, more vital element in human affairs.

To understand what is being built now, it is useful to step back and study Gehry's early proposals for activating the AGO's north edge, which programmatically included adding gallery space and changing the entrance and adjacent retail space. Gehry initially proposed two major moves: re-establishing the main entry on the axis of Walker Court and adding major volumes along Dundas. One of the early architectural models shows a series of five lively tower elements dancing along the street, some coloured silver-grey, some bronze-brown (fig. 6). White drapery-like planes sail off the tops of the central entry

Fig. 6

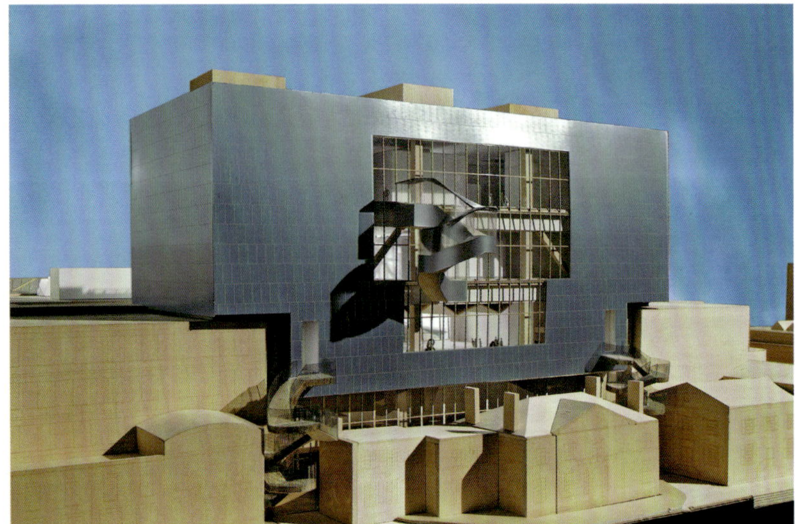

Fig. 7

View of architectural model of an earlier, later abandoned scheme for the AGO, along Dundas Street West, July 2003

View of architectural model for the AGO, looking northeast from Grange Park, April 2004

Courtesy of Gehry Partners, LLP

tower and also from a new volume at the east end. A transparent, second-level walkway threads in and out of the tower elements, this energetic ensemble bracketed by the mute, concrete-clad Parkin additions of 1974 and 1977 at the far east and west ends.

Gehry was enthused with this approach. The thoughtful jumble of tower-boxes is reminiscent of his Massachusetts Institute of Technology's Ray and Maria Stata Center, which he had just completed in 2003. The drapery-like elements recall his perfected manipulations of light-catching, sculpted planes in recent projects such as the Guggenheim Museum in Bilbao and the Walt Disney Concert Hall in Los Angeles. However, to insert the large towers into the existing AGO building fabric and provide the necessary foundations and sub-structure would have added many millions of dollars to the total project cost. Primarily for cost reasons, the towers along Dundas scheme was abandoned.

In the fall of 2003 Gehry rethought the project. He generated a sweeping, horizontal concept for the Dundas edge, keeping some of the new gallery space of the previously imagined towers, but shifting most of it to a single volume at the south Grange Park side (fig. 7). For the Dundas stretch, he created a curving, slanting, twisting Douglas fir structure that supports and encases the glazed sculpture promenade on the second floor. This dramatic, 425-foot-long (129.5 m) internal space provides additional passage to the AGO's north galleries and also a large new doorway into the existing Henry Moore Sculpture Centre (fig. 8).

The main structure of the sculpture promenade is built up of huge, exposed wood members, 10 1/2 inch x 19 1/2 inch (26.5 cm x 49.5 cm) in cross-section that from the midpoint of the structure lean and flow east and west, supporting panels of clear glass. At the ends, toward McCaul and Beverley streets, the windshield-like array extends beyond the promenade, bends and breaks apart, turning toward the sidestreets to make what Gehry calls "billboards." At the east end, the termination of the promenade and the flipping outward and upward of the billboard element create a handsome new outdoor space for the existing Henry Moore sculpture, *Large Two Forms*.

The plastic, spatial performance along Dundas will, in its concave and convex sculpting, draw the space of the street into the AGO and vice-versa (fig. 9). It will accelerate the street space linearly from the colourful cacophony of Chinese shops to the west to the grandeur of University Avenue to the east. Its canopy will also create a welcoming, covered arcade. The glazed façade will functionally support overhead wires for the Toronto Transit Commission streetcars, a small gesture that serves to further underscore the

Fig. 8

Fig. 9

AGO's intention to reach out and connect to the city.

During a visit with Gehry at his Los Angeles office, he was eager to discuss with me the Dundas canopy and promenade and his long-time use of wood construction: "Deciding to go with the wood structure for the AGO was a big deal. I loved Alvar Aalto and his use of wood. Still, for me, he's the best humanist, because it's a kind of laid back, casual humanism, whereas Frank Lloyd Wright was very formal and impositional." Gehry continued to talk enthusiastically about the importance of wood and how it had evolved in his own work,

> In the 1976 Norton Simon house in Malibu, Norton let me do two layers of wood for the trellis but I really didn't know how to do it. I wanted several more layers. Then, just after that, while doing studies for my own Santa Monica house, I piled up a bunch of sticks, and it looked like the wind whipped it up. These experiments were about wood but more about trying to get a sense of movement. I think with the AGO the use of wood is very Canadian…it must be my Canadian side.[8]

In fact Gehry's imaginative use of wood construction can be traced back to 1963 and his Kay Jewelers offices and warehouse in Los Angeles, where influences from traditional Japanese architecture, Frank Lloyd Wright and Rudolph Schlinder are evidenced.[9] But it is in his own extraordinary house in Santa Monica in 1978 – a work that has become iconic – that we see Gehry conceptually breaking out of the pre-existing bungalow box with an angular, wood framed window-skylight above the kitchen (figs. 10–12), which seems to predict, twenty-eight years earlier, the bold, block-long breaking out of the box along Dundas Street. Gehry's deployment of wood has become increasingly sophisticated, reaching a zenith in the magnificent wood-lined interior of his 2003 Walt Disney Concert Hall.

Perhaps most telling of Gehry's love of gutsy wood framing is his current design exploration for a new house in Venice for himself and his wife, Berta, composed of a series of pavilions set in a walled courtyard. The primary pavilion will be constructed of densely assembled Canadian Douglas fir components that are 12 inch x 12 inch in cross-section. Interestingly, the models and drawings for his new home evolved in his studio directly alongside ongoing work on the AGO in Toronto, his first home. Just outside the studio, in the parking lot, Gehry's design staff constructed a full-scale mock-up of the Canadian Douglas fir structure for Frank and Berta's new house, and one can sense its close relationship

Fig. 10

Fig. 11

Fig. 12

to the Art Gallery of Ontario's wood structure.

Intentionally exaggerated in its horizontal sweep, the dynamism of the AGO's Dundas Street façade is gathered and pulled through Walker Court, and launched vertically through the new south volume hovering over The Grange and Grange Park. This south element houses the banquet hall and new contemporary galleries. The redirection of space upward from Walker Court is achieved with an elaborate, highly sculptural "stair-performance." This kind of architectural elaboration has become one of Gehry's favourite devices to activate space, give scale, provide social encounters, and lead visitors on mysterious journeys. Indeed, Gehry's fifty-foot spiralling staircase for Walker Court combines both baroque and early modernist sensibilities. May we imagine it as flowing from a magnificent collision between Gianlorenzo Bernini's 1624–33 Baldachin in St. Peter's and Constantin Brancusi's 1930s *King of Kings* sculpture?

Like his passion for wood construction, Gehry's intelligent games with stairs extend throughout his career. From the breaking-out stairs of the 1976–79 Gemini G.E.L. project and the wavy stairs-to-nowhere of the 1982 Beverley Hills Civic Centre competition to the staircase of the Loyola University Law School's Fritz B. Burns Academic Center of 1981–84 (fig. 13), which one critic calls a "fluid emanation," [10] we can see the importance of stairs for Gehry, not just as means of circulation and large-scale decoration but as moments of exhilaration and near-flight.

Sitting with me in his Los Angeles office, Gehry talked about his preoccupation with movement in architecture and also with natural light:

> The big issue of movement came to me way back when I was doing Norton Simon's house. I talked with him a lot about movement and how to express movement. Then I did it on my Santa Monica house. The sketches from then [of the skylight-window breaking out] show it. I'm also very conscious of light. Project to project my manipulation of it is pretty much the same everywhere, but the quality shifts, so you have to change the material. I'm very conscious of that.  It rains a lot in Bilbao but we have very bright light in Los Angeles. There are a million ways to finish aluminum and titanium. At the AGO I'm bending the light on the Dundas, glass side. Then I use titanium, which gets nice with age, and do a sky thing on the Grange Park side.[11]

Then Gehry paused and pulled my notepad in front of him, doing a pair of quick sketches of one of the new Thomson galleries in an area of the AGO that he is renovating (fig. 14):

Fig. 13

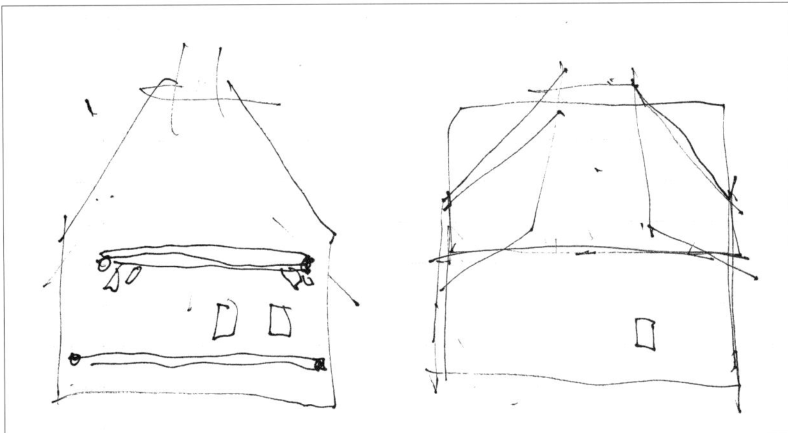



Fig. 14

> The Thomson galleries are very tall. I wanted to
> make two levels but the foundations couldn't take
> the extra weight, so we had to go with one storey.
> The problem is scale. The spaces are tall, with
> light coming from big skylights, but the works of
> art in the Thomson collection are mostly small. So
> I'm trying to figure out how to add things to scale
> down the space, like a rail around the walls. [12]

These sketches of one of the 34-foot-high Thomson
galleries reveal Gehry's central concern with the art
objects and how people will experience them – issues
of movement, light and scale. During the early fall of
2005, Gehry and AGO staff constructed temporary,
full-size mock-ups of various Thomson galleries,
experimenting with wall materials, lighting, vitrine
design and a waist-height rail around the perimeter.
The contemplative experience of the grand, yet
intimate Thomson galleries will contrast with the

exhilarating experience of Walker Court, which, with
its modernist-baroque staircase, sweeps one upward
visually and physically to the hovering south volume.

After abandoning the towers along Dundas scheme,
which was difficult for Gehry, he struggled in particular
with the development and articulation of the south
volume. About his decision to clad it in blue titanium
panels, Gehry commented, "Yes, sky-blue…I've tried
to make the thing go away. I fought it for a while. But
now I'm happy with it because the south façade facing
Grange Park will dematerialize a bit. And my box will go
with Alsop's OCAD box."[13] In fact, the height of the two
boxes, from ground level to top, will be almost identical.

The south volume is efficient in its rectangular
dumb-boxness and alluring at the same time. The
sky-blue box will visually terminate the axis of John
Street. It seems impossible not to think of Gehry's early
experiments in manipulating simple boxes, perhaps the
first being in hiss Faith Plating Company project of 1964,
which he calls his "initial encounter with an articulate
dumb box."[14] Other encounters followed such as the
O'Neill Hay Barn of 1968, where Gehry created a simple
rectangular enclosure clad in corrugated metal, with a
roof that is tilted between diagonal corners. He said of
the project that "the reflections of the sky on the metal
make the building disappear sometimes,"[15] a remark
that comes full circle in his desire for the AGO box to

disappear into the Toronto sky. Equally interesting in
Gehry's history of sophisticated box-making is the ice-
blue stucco volume of his 1973 Cochiti Lake Town Center
which "melds the form with the distant mountains."[16]

The interior of the south tower is another story,
because once visitors ascend to the top of this
"hill" overlooking Grange Park, they will discover a
spatially intricate sub-village of tall contemporary
galleries, showered with natural light from above.
The architectural section of the building here is
complex, with a series of flexible galleries on the top
two floors – the fourth and fifth – that promise to be one
of the most rewarding parts of the AGO transformation.

The contemporary galleries are arranged as tight
clusters of one-room buildings, a compositional
strategy that has preoccupied Gehry as far back as
1986. In the winter of 1986, while talking about his
relationship with art and artists, Gehry reflected
on still lifes and the lessons for him in the work of
Giorgio Morandi, Paul Cézanne and Henri Matisse:

> When I started doing one-room buildings…I started
> seeing Morandi in a different way, and then
> I started looking at Cézanne's still lifes, and other
> still lifes, in a different way than I had. I'd always
> looked at them as a total composition. And now I
> started looking at the pieces as individual pieces,

and at their relationships to each other, and then
the spaces between them – which made it possible
for me to see Matisse's cut-outs differently.
I didn't get them before. I remember seeing them
when he was doing them, and I thought, 'The
guy's off the end.' But now I've started to see
the singular pieces playing off each other – it's
object next to object – and they're so beautiful,
because you sense the hands-on, the cut of this
masterful scissor cutting through the thing, quietly,
effortlessly. I hope when I'm that age – he was in
his seventies – I can do something like that. [17]

Twenty years after these remarks, if one studies the
floor plans and sections of the clustered rooms of the
contemporary galleries, it appears that Gehry continues
to think in terms of still lifes – assembling objects next
to objects. In terms of precedent, one can see, hear
and feel the success of his 1983 Los Angeles Museum
of Contemporary Art's Temporary Contemporary
(now The Geffen Contemporary) when Gehry talks
about the AGO. He maintains that like the Temporary
Contemporary, "the AGO should not overwhelm…can't
be too pristine [and] must generate great relationships
between the galleries, the art and the city."[18]

Indeed the architectural section of the south block
is intriguing – shells of space within larger spaces

Fig.15

within yet grander spaces. This series of galleries-at-the-top promises to be one of the most beautiful parts of Gehry's conception – a sphere of spatial-social activation flowing from the city, within and through the AGO, and back out into the city. Akin to the formal operations of Cubism, the architect's spatial folding and layering have become highly developed, enabling his dynamic architectural framing of both high-end cultural production and everyday life.

## Zoomorphic Antecedents

Frank Gehry's obsessions with zoomorphic forms, from fish to fowl, are well known. In 1980 he drew an eagle-like entry for a Chicago Tribune Tower ideas competition. He created snake and fish lamps made from Formica chips in 1983, followed by a 6.7-metre-high glass fish at the Walker Art Center in Minneapolis. Later he designed fish buildings in Kobe and Barcelona. Sometimes these animal visions are cheery and happy; other times dark and sinister.

Frank himself has retold the story many times of his youthful curiosity, when his maternal grandmother would bring a carp home from Toronto's Kensington Market and keep it in the bathtub before making gefilte fish. In the lobby of his 1989 Chiat/Day Toronto advertising agency project, he placed an old bathtub on the entry axis and plopped a lead fish in it.[19] Gehry acknowledges his "aha" zoomorphic moment when he began making the snake-inspired staircase for the Vitra Design Museum.[20]

Numerous writers on Gehry have attempted to explain his gravitation to zoomorphic forms. Kurt Forster believes that for Gehry the fish represents a perfect creature — a symbol of the perfection that he strives to attain in his architecture.[21] Germano Celant claims that "the snake, like the fish, is a symbol of love and libido in Gehry's work."[22] Perhaps it is the power of the primitive. Whatever the explanation, the Art Gallery of Ontario is fortunate to be the recipient of a family of six orgiastic animal forms, dispersed by the architect throughout the project: the skeletal glass fish swimming along Dundas; the snake-like entry ramp that connects the two lobby levels; the orgulous, coiling Walker Court staircase; the "barnacle" external stairs attached to the south façade of the south volume; and a pair of worm-like emergency egress staircases that curl down from the same volume and land in Grange Park.

In Gehry's provocative 1983 folly design *The Prison* (fig. 15), the most basic zoomorphic ingredients of the future AGO can be seen. In this proposal (accompanied by a rather preposterous story about an estate and a burglar who becomes a prisoner there), two remarkable forms are presented: a prison, shaped like a coiled snake and constructed of brick, and a glass fish pavilion.[23] On close inspection, the fish pavilion — scales removed from its mid-section to expose a structural skeleton — has an eerie likeness to the similarly ribbed canopy and sculpture promenade that will stretch along Dundas Street. Although squat in comparison, the coiled snake prison of 1983 seems to be ready to spiral upward as the majestic Walker Court staircase.

Of course difficulty arises when my description of the Walker Court staircase as a collision between Bernini and Brancusi intersects with that of a spiralling snake. The resulting hybrid conjures images, memories and fantasies shooting in a thousand directions, but that is the kind of richness of imagery and democratizing of spatial and social possibility that Frank Gehry seeks — a negation of any single definition or finalizing ideology, preferring instead multiple interpretations. This was one of the intentions and results of Cubism and, in part, what made it revolutionary.[24] Similar to the world of Cubism and its destruction of absolutes, Gehry's work thrives on and promotes the relativity of modern values.

The AGO's zoomorphic elements will be crucial actors in the institution's rebirth, interrupting everyday life as art itself does, to intentionally complicate and confront, but also to propel us toward new discoveries, new revelations.

**Pentimento**

In Sydney Pollack's recent documentary film *Sketches of Frank Gehry*, Frank talks about the magic of art and mentions his envy of painters. He says he wishes he was a painter.[25] He has acknowledged that his process as an architect is akin to that of a sculptor; but surely it is equally like that of a painter, brushing on layer after layer, manipulating form, space, texture, colour and light.

The challenge is particularly acute when Gehry's "canvas" already has an old painting on it. This is the case with the Art Gallery of Ontario, where an agglomeration of buildings evolved over a century, along with a number of additions and renovations. As architect-artist, Gehry had to selectively overpaint, painstakingly deciding what to leave, what to erase, what to add, what to allow to show through – and at this layering, he is masterful.

The public tends to think of Gehry as the creator of entirely new, stand-alone structures, which emerged from a blank canvas. True, some of his most acclaimed works such as the Guggenheim in Bilbao and the Walt Disney Concert Hall in Los Angeles are new buildings, but a careful review of the hundreds of realized and unrealized projects completed since he started his own firm in 1962 reveals that Gehry has frequently worked with preexisting buildings and messy contexts. Both the Los Angeles Museum of Contemporary Art's Temporary Contemporary (formerly a L.A. police car garage) and his own famous "house within a house" in Santa Monica are prime examples. To say the least, he is both experienced and comfortable with radically reworking and adding to existing buildings under difficult conditions such as those he found at the Art Gallery of Ontario.

There is something extraordinary about the way that Frank Gehry labours, back and forth, between the old and the new. He seems to conceptually excavate, sometimes digging deep, sometimes barely scratching the surface. Along Dundas Street he will radically reshape not only that side of the Gallery, but also the space of the street itself. With the south volume, here too he was not timid, creating a bold blue box that will both celebrate and converse with Will Alsop's pixilated "table top" nearby.

In Walker Court Gehry respects that dignified space at the heart of the institution while simultaneously threading through mysterious new walkways behind its arcade and blasting a new staircase up its south face. In contrast with these deep moves, he barely touches the Henry Moore Sculpture Centre, gently articulating a new north doorway into the sculpture promenade along Dundas. As well, he remains respectful of the historic Grange house by lightly framing it with new elements above it and to the sides.

As a child Frank Gehry first experienced art at the Art Gallery of Ontario with his mother and now, many decades later, he is seeing it all again. Layering new architecture on the old, he is allowing us to see the old in an entirely new way. Moreover, there is a gentle humanizing in the word *pentimento* – the sense of a painter "repenting" and changing his mind – which entails transparency and a long-term view of history and time. Ultimately, it is not just form, space and scale that Gehry understands and manipulates so well as an architect but also and, more significantly, time. His is a very big picture of time, understanding the fragility of the world and the necessity of striving for a shared sense of community – for cooperation and tolerance. It is his way of seeing the world and Toronto, where his own time started, growing up on Dundas Street West. ■

## Endnotes

The epigraph to this essay is drawn from Lillian Hellman, *Pentimento* (New York: Little, Brown and Company, 1973), 1, quoted in Peter Arnell and Ted Bickford, eds., *Frank Gehry: Buildings and Projects* (New York: Rizzoli, 1985), 16.

1  "Transformation AGO: Art Gallery of Ontario Expansion," GMP, issue 21, vol. 1: Architectural (August 1, 2005): Gehry International, Inc., AO-2.5.

2  Frank Gehry interview with author, Los Angeles, California, November 29, 2005.

3  Ibid.

4  The Ontario College of Art and Design's Sharp Centre for Design was designed by Alsop Architects Ltd. and Robbie/Young + Wright Architects and opened in 2004.

5  Melvin Charney's *Other Monuments, 1970–77* was presented at the Art Gallery of Ontario from March 4 to April 30, 1978, in the McLean Gallery and on the north side of the AGO along Dundas Street West. Box location: D-4-10-4, Edward P. Taylor Research Library and Archives, Art Gallery of Ontario.

6  Amy Goldin, "Report from Toronto and Montreal," *Art in America* 65 (March/April 1977): 43.

7  Andy Patton, "Artists Review" [on Melvin Charney], *Artists Cooperative Toronto* (ACT), April 30, 1978, 12.

8  Frank Gehry, interview with author, Los Angeles, California, August 26, 2005.

9  Peter Arnell and Ted Bickford, eds., *Frank Gehry: Buildings and Projects* (New York: Rizzoli, 1985), 22–23.

10  Arnell and Bickford, *Frank Gehry*, 13.

11  Frank Gehry interview, August 26, 2005.

12  Ibid.

13  Ibid.

14  Arnell and Bickford, *Frank Gehry*, 24–25.

15  Ibid., 40–41

16  Ibid., 70–73.

17  Adele Freedman, *Sight Lines: Looking at Architecture and Design in Canada* (Toronto: Oxford University Press, 1990), 68.

18  Comments by Frank Gehry at the AGO, Toronto, January 28, 2004; also in Larry Wayne Richards, "Returning to the Original Gehry," *Art Gallery of Ontario Members' Journal* 13, no. 1 (Winter 2005): 12–13.

19  Larry Richards, "Mocking-up Life: Chiat/Day Offices, Toronto," *The Canadian Architect* 34, no. 5 (May 1989): 26–33.

20  Frank Gehry interview, August 26, 2005.

21  Kurt Forster, "Architectural Choreography" in Dal Co and Forster, *Frank O. Gehry: The Complete Works* (New York: Monacelli Press, 1998), 21.

22  Germano Celant, "Reflections on Frank Gehry" in Arnell and Bickford, Frank Gehry, 12.

23  Arnell and Bickford, Frank Gehry, 268–69.

24  H.H. Arnason, *History of Modern Art* (New York: Harry N. Abrams, 1986), 164.

25  *Sketches of Frank Gehry*, directed by Sydney Pollack (2005; Los Angeles, CA).

We decided that the most appropriate vehicle would be an advanced seminar with a dual focus.

# In School with Frank Gehry

George Baird

The Faculty of Architecture, Landscape and Design at the University of Toronto has a long-standing relationship with Frank Gehry, beginning many years ago with his first public lecture in Toronto, and culminating five years ago in the creation of the International Visiting Chair in Architectural Design, named in his honour, in our faculty. So it was no surprise for me to receive an invitation from the AGO's Matthew Teitelbaum, Michael and Sonja Koerner director, and CEO, and Dennis Reid, director, Collections & Research, and senior curator of Canadian Art, for my faculty to participate in the preparations for the Frank Gehry exhibition.

We decided that the most appropriate vehicle would be an advanced seminar with a dual focus. On the one hand, it would look at a number of recent projects from the Gehry office that were planned to form part of the exhibition; on the other, it would explore a series of strategies to display and interpret the projects in the exhibition itself.

Thus it was last spring that Dennis Reid and myself met once a week with a group of twelve graduate students from the Faculty of Architecture, Landscape and Design to explore possible approaches to the projects and to the exhibition together. Interestingly enough, our discussions also benefitted from guest appearances by three additional members of the faculty, all of whom, at earlier stages of their own careers, had worked in the Gehry office. Tom Bessai, An Te Liu and Michael Mantzoris had each spent a year or so working there, and had even participated in the work on some of the projects that formed the subjects of both the seminar and the exhibition.

We explored the projects from many different points of view. We looked at them programmatically, discovering with some surprise how frequently Gehry had worked on similar projects at earlier stages in his own career. Chicago's Millennium Park, for example, has behind it earlier designs for other outdoor performance stages, including a number of projects for renovations to the Hollywood Bowl. We attempted to track the influence on Gehry's designs of the work of other earlier architects, whose work he admires, such as Alvar Aalto, Hans Scharoun, Charles Moore and Aldo Rossi. We noted the complex crossovers in the development of his characteristic architectural language between architecture and art – especially that of the California artists with whom he has long been associated. Then, too, we attempted to identify characteristic formal themes in the work: oppositions between normative and aberrant elements, compositions that sometimes appear to be the result of the fragmentation of an originary, unitary volume and sometimes that

of a still-life grouping of distinct elements.

Another group of students in the seminar sought to devise effective exhibition techniques for the display and interpretation of the projects. For example, we developed a graphic design for a catalogue; we explored an approach to the exhibition that employed characteristic recent Gehry-esque spatial geometries to display his work; and we developed an interactive design methodology that attempted to integrate his characteristic formal language into design by children.

At the end of the academic term, the students' projects were presented to a group of staff from the AGO, who were starting work on the exhibition proper, and the results elicited lively discussion. Curator Dennis Reid, the twelve students and I found being in school with Frank Gehry a rewarding experience indeed. ■

Maybe the year before they were modelling a stealth fighter, but here they were now, resolving the intersection of two double-curved surfaces so that the entryway to an art museum could be that much more beautifu

# Model Employee

An Te Liu

It was 1993, and one day I received a call from the office of Frank Gehry. I frantically assembled a portfolio of my work, went in for an interview, and the next morning I found myself working on the biggest model I had ever laid eyes on. Like so many before and after me, I was now an intern at FOGA (as it was then called), and my primary job was to make models. Model making is the lifeblood of Gehry's design process. Often we would wear lab coats and white respirators while working. We might have passed for doctors, if we weren't also covered in sawdust and hardened bits of hot glue. At that time Bilbao was in design development and there was a nonstop parade in and out of the cramped woodshop, each model maker cradling their own peculiar basswood chunk of Bilbao, which they were shaping on a huge belt sander nicknamed "Big Boy." The sight was both inspiring and somewhat amusing. Invariably they would be asked by people working on other projects, "What is that?" or "Where does it go?" and "Which way is up with that thing?" A few years later we all found out the answers, in life-size.

Our physical, or so-called analog models, were aided by drawings and templates made by the CATIA software experts in the office. Rumour had it that some of the CATIA people came from the aeronautics field and ended up at FOGA after military spending cutbacks wiped out jobs at Lockheed Martin and places like that. Personally, I loved the idea that we had these converted rocket scientists in an architecture office. Maybe the year before they were modelling a stealth fighter, but here they were now, resolving the intersection of two double-curved surfaces so that the entryway to an art museum could be that much more beautiful.

Building designs would often begin with a sketch, which was then fleshed out in a number of rough models; they would become more refined models and at this point the design would enter the digital realm. There would always be a constant exchange between virtual and real models – the latest version of a design might be described in a CATIA model, the drawings from which would be used to build the latest physical model. Modifications, often quite dramatic, would be made to the physical model, and then the changes would be incorporated into a new CATIA model. Sometimes a digital arm would be used to plot the modifications directly from the modified model, which might appear rather battle-scarred after all that was done to it. And so this iterative process would continue – one in which the eye, the hand and the machine were all equal partners in the creation and refinement of form and space.

When a flurry of model making was finished, Frank would come down and meet with his senior partners in front of the models. They would spend a long time just looking, peering from every angle and getting their heads right inside the models. This process reminded me of a documentary I once saw on the fashion designer Yohji Yamamoto. In one scene he is staring intently at a new dress being modelled before him, gently pulling at the fabric. This goes on for some time and then, all of a sudden, he pulls out a big pair of scissors and just starts cutting the dress up, searching for a better shape. He looks and then he responds, and this is what Frank did. He would not hesitate to hack up a model that we had just spent hundreds of hours building. Frank has a great sculptural eye, but at the root of it, and despite the seeming strangeness of his forms, he also possesses a great sense of scale and accommodation. In scanning the models, he was looking for just the right kind of spaces and experiences, and he would keep cutting, pulling and bending until he found them.

After long days of making and re-making, we would sometimes find the ideal release – we played street hockey. For this we used the motorcycle testing cage at the DMV right beside the office. It was perfect, although to those Canadians among us, it seemed a bit odd playing hockey beneath the shade of palm trees. One night Frank decided to join us, showing up in a Toronto Maple Leafs jersey. His presence lent both an air of excitement and caution to the game. Whenever he had the ball, it seemed we would all play a little more gingerly and clear just a tiny bit of space for him. I'd say we weren't being pandering though – it just didn't seem right to lay a big body check on one the greatest architects of our time. ■

One could not help but
feel we were a part of
history in the making.

Michael Mantzoris

A decade has passed since my time spent working in the offices of Frank O. Gehry and Associates (FOGA), as the firm was known then, for a period of over two and a half years as a summer graduate student in 1993. The office was staffed at around eighty people including support staff – the largest office I had ever worked at. At the suggestion of a Southern California Institute of Architecture (SCI-Arc) instructor, who taught photograms and worked at FOGA, I was invited to come in for an interview. Ironically I got the interview on the merits of my darkroom work rather than my studio work. I had been able to transform a copper fabric projected onto photo emulsion paper – essentially painting with a small flashlight, which made the images quite captivating. What the office was looking for in an intern, outside of the obvious, was a sensibility to interpret and reconfigure the limits of a given and be able to understand it as process.

That first summer was spent working on the models for the Walt Disney Concert Hall. The design had been developed to the interior and exterior confirmation models. Attempting to realize a scaled accuracy was challenging and at times seemed impossible. At that point the building was to be clad in stone. The patterning of stone was all resolved with the computer and, to my understanding, the trick was to replace where possible compound curves with simple ones by manipulating the material in one direction. Though deadlines seemed imminent, they always came with a sense of calm through an exhaustive investigation of the design. At times the process could be described as iterative, sometimes representational, but always rigorous and informed by corporeal tectonics.

Parametric modelling, a CAD system designed to track and integrate geometric parameters set by the modeller, enables analog models to be represented and manipulated in a digital environment. In the case of FOGA, this language was continually referenced and refined from analog (sketch) model to digital model and back to analog (confirmation) model. By means of this modelling, however present in the process, a meaningful tool was applied in an overall strategy that made it possible for a new architecture to be realized, as witnessed through the construction of Bilbao and Disney.

For most, the office culture was really centred by and on the creative act. The two moments that stand out during my tenure came in the winter of 1994/95 on the Berlin Museum competition and the redesign of the Peter B. Lewis residence in Lyndhurst, Ohio. The former was an Edwin Chan production, a contextually concise interpretation for an under-published competition for major addition/reconstruction of the Neues Museum next to Schinkel 's Altes Museum. The 1994 L.A. earthquake had hit during the last days of the competition, but the entry was made in total heroic fashion. The latter came during the redesign of the Lewis residence. The project had been around for a while, and I had worked on a previous scheme with another designer. It was now Craig Webb's project, with whom I had previously worked on the Disney interiors. The imagery of High Renaissance sculptures of flowing fabric carved out of solid marble had been circulating through the office for a while but seeing it come to fruition was exhilarating. Craig and the design team had used red felt fabric encrusted with honey wax to transgress these simplified forms, thus creating a phenomenal artificial topography. The "horse's head," as it would be called, found its form, and a completely new language had been introduced to my vocabulary. The office by this point started looking like a cabinet of architectural curiosities. One could not help but feel we were a part of history in the making. ∎

The design processes of this period were characterized by outlandish physical models and unbridled variety in formal, material and technical exploration.

# Refinements in Radical Form-making: The View from within Gehry's Office, 1999–2001

Tom Bessai

## Experimentation

In the mid-1990s the Gehry office underwent a period of extraordinary experimentation in design and production techniques. The Guggenheim Museum Bilbao was constructed; the unbuilt Lewis House lent its iconic "horse's head" to the Experience Music Project in Seattle and the DZ Bank in Berlin. The broad strokes of a formal and procedural agenda for the office were established: the use of complex iterative physical models in design; the technical/digital development of strategies for the documentation and construction of buildings dominated by curved geometries. The design processes of this period were characterized by outlandish physical models and unbridled variety in formal, material and technical exploration. The first indications from the construction sites were that the exuberant projects were in fact technically feasible and spatially rich.

## Emergence

I had moved to L.A. to do a graduate degree at UCLA in 1998. In the leading academic studios of UCLA and SCI-Arc, Greg Lynn, Karl Chu and others were promoting formal experimentation in pure digital design. A consensus was building around emergent digital practices, co-opting the algorithms of animation and mathematics software for the production of smooth and mutable architectural surfaces and environments. Despite obvious formal congruency with the Gehry work, there seemed to be some resistance to direct association with his office on conceptual grounds: Gehry's work was seen as a fundamentally analog practice producing sculptural physical objects and using the computer exclusively for documentation. The popular success of the 1990s built work perhaps contributed to its dismissal in academic circles. At UCLA, in particular, generative concepts were strictly digital. Physical by-products of digital designs were typically generated directly from machine processes. I was drawn to the Gehry studio, to explore possible alliances between theoretical digital techniques and construction/fabrication.

**Rationalization**

From approximately the spring of 1999 until the fall of 2001, I worked under Craig Webb on the design for MIT's Ray and Maria Stata Center, the Millennium Park Music Pavilion (now the Jay Pritzker Pavilion) in Chicago, the Walt Disney Concert Hall in L.A. and other projects. There were many compelling aspects to working in the studio, not least of which was the lively internal discourse surrounding the work. The culture of the office had changed substantially since Bilbao and the Lewis House. What had seemed a few years before to be impossibly difficult and obscure design methods had been tested and proven to be viable. With this confidence and in light of performance and cost information from the first generation of built "complex form" projects, the emphasis in the office had matured into a focus upon refinement of technique. Experimentation was still pervasive, but it had narrowed in scope from the willful sculptural form-making of the previous generation of projects to a more controlled exploration of form and methods. Specific techniques had been put in place for quickly creating, modifying and rationalizing curved and faceted building elements that could be confidently converted to digital models and to construction assemblies. We were thoroughly trained in these techniques. Curvature tolerances and panelization were driving themes in the design development work on MIT, Chicago, and many other projects. The architectural forms and systems being created were closely aligned with the specific tools of production, both analog and digital. I have carried on with this principle in my own design work and into my teaching.

**Fabrication**

Today the work of the Gehry office continues to evolve. Current practices accept broader integration of scaled, rapid prototypes into physical models. With the establishment of Gehry Technologies, academic "digital skepticism" has given way to collaboration as common interests in parametric modelling lead to new and productive alliances. ▪

# Contributors

Gillian MacKay is a Toronto-based freelance arts writer and a contributing editor to *Canadian Art* magazine.

Dennis Reid is director of Collections and Research and senior curator of Canadian Art at the Art Gallery of Ontario.

Larry Wayne Richards is professor of Architecture in the Faculty of Architecture, Landscape and Design at the University of Toronto.

George Baird is dean of the Faculty of Architecture, Landscape and Design at the University of Toronto.

An Te Liu is an artist, whose work is exhibited internationally. He is associate professor in the Faculty of Architecture, Landscape and Design at the University of Toronto.

Michael Mantzoris, M. Arch, OAA, MRAIC, lives and practices architecture in Toronto.

Tom Bessai is an adjunct professor at the Faculty of Architecture, Landscape and Design at the University of Toronto and principal of Denegri Bessai Studio.